PSHE & CITIZENSHIP

FOR AGES 7-9

Choices

Decisions

Opinions

Negotiations

Dilemmas

Finding out

Planning

MOLLY POTTER

Published 2008 by A & C Black Publishers Ltd
38 Soho Square, London W1D 3HB

www.acblack.com

Dedicated to Sylvia Allen

ISBN 978-0-7136-8979-2

Written by Molly Potter
Design by Cathy Tincknell
Illustration by Mike Phillips

Copyright © Molly Potter 2008

Printed in Great Britain by Martins the Printers, Berwick-on- Tweed

This book is produced using paper that is made from wood grown in
managed, sustainable forests. It is natural, renewable and recyclable.
The logging and manufacturing processes conform to the
environmental regulations of the country of origin.

To see our full range of books visit
www.acblack.com

CONTENTS

What is PSHE and Citizenship?

Personal, Social and Health Education and Citizenship is an exciting part of the curriculum that aims to equip children and young people with the knowledge, skills, attitudes and values that will help them to make positive decisions in their lives. PSHE and Citizenship is often taught in discrete lessons but can equally well be a main feature of other lessons across the school curriculum and can be strongly connected with school ethos.

The aims of PSHE

The DCSF's framework for PSHE is non-statutory and consequently there can be some flexibility in how your school programme is structured and which areas you prioritise. This also enables your school to adjust its PSHE policy to meet the needs of your pupils in your particular setting. This book covers many learning objectives in the non-statutory PSHE curriculum and can be used to enhance any existing PSHE scheme of work. The activities can also be used to complement the SEAL curriculum and provide an alternative way of covering some of its learning objectives.

In developing your programme it might be helpful to start with the 'big picture' and consider what it is you hope to achieve with your PSHE curriculum. Your aims might include some or all of the following.

For children and young people:

★ To have developed a sense of self-worth and confidence.
★ To have developed their own individual moral framework.
★ To be emotionally literate – including an ability to empathise with others.
★ To view their future with aspiration.
★ To have effective communication skills, including assertiveness.
★ To be able to have positive relationships with others.
★ To have an awareness of prejudice and the harm it can cause.
★ To celebrate diversity and know that every individual has similar needs, rights and responsibilities.
★ To know how to, and be inclined to, make healthy choices.
★ To make informed choices.
★ To understand and avoid unnecessary risk of harm.
★ To have a discerning eye for the messages in the media.
★ To have an awareness and a responsibility towards local and global issues.
★ To know how to access help and support and how to protect themselves.

Why use this book?

Inspirational ideas: PSHE and Citizenship is full of engaging and thought provoking activities that span the information, skills, attitudes and values elements of PSHE. The activities will stimulate discussion and help pupils to explore a variety of issues through active learning, which is deemed good practice in all PSHE Guidance. Many of the activities also have cross-curricular links and need not be reserved solely for PSHE e.g. some activities lend themselves easily to writing for different purposes such as persuasive writing or journalistic writing and many activities fit very well into the current drive for 'Speaking and Listening' in schools.

How the book is organised

This book has been split into five sections:

★ Self-esteem and self-awareness
★ A focus on relationships
★ Exploring attitudes and values
★ Health and safety issues
★ The world around us

In the first part of each section there are teacher's notes for all of the activities. These notes outline the purpose of each activity and give key points to help you introduce concepts and guide discussions. These notes also include interesting and fun extension activities that can expand the exploration of each issue considerably. In whatever way to choose this book, whether as a focus for your school policy or as a 'dip in' resource, its fresh approach to the 'same old' learning objectives will hopefully make the delivery of PSHE more interesting for you and for your pupils!

SELF-ESTEEM AND SELF-AWARENESS

YOU ARE UNIQUE! (PAGE 8)

Purpose of the activity: To highlight the fact that everyone is unique and to celebrate diversity!

Key discussion points

★ No two people (in the world) are likely to complete the sheet in the same way.

★ The fact that we are all different makes the world a more interesting place. It would be very boring if we were all exactly the same.

★ People generally like to be asked questions about themselves. Asking a person questions shows that you are interested in them.

Extension activities

Pupils could:

★ make up a similar sheet for other people to fill in.

★ make up a set of questions that can only be answered by looking at each others' sheets.

★ investigate other ways in which they are different from each other.

★ see how few yes/no questions would be needed to split the class into individuals e.g. are you female? (splits the class in two). Do you like fish fingers? (could split the class into 4) and so on...

WONDERFUL ME! (PAGE 9)

Purpose of activity: To boost self esteem and increase self awareness.

Key discussion points

★ Most people enjoy being asked about themselves as we generally like people to take an interest in us.

★ Difference and diversity is great and needs to be celebrated! Each person will have filled in the form differently.

Extension activities

★ After pupils have filled in the sheet with their answers, the teacher could make a 'quiz' – the answers to which can be found on the completed pupils' sheets. The sheets could then be stuck around the room and each pupil could be given the quiz and asked to hunt for the answers.

★ Pupils could try to guess how their friends might have answered some of the questions on the sheet as a way of sharing information about themselves.

YOUR STRENGTHS (PAGE 10)

Purpose of activity: To increase self-awareness and self-esteem.

Key discussion points

★ Because pupils have to make a choice, they have to be positive about something they might feel they are not very good at. If pupils cannot do or have not done either of the choices e.g. playing a musical instrument or speaking another language, ask them to tick the one they think they would be best at.

★ In this country, if we celebrate our achievements and declare anything about ourselves that we are proud of it can be interpreted as 'boasting.' This can make boosting self-esteem difficult!

★ It is wonderful that everyone has different strengths.

Extension activities

★ You could explore the idea of multiple intelligences: word intelligence, logic and maths intelligence, musical intelligence, nature intelligence, spiritual intelligence, body intelligence, spatial awareness intelligence, people intelligence and self intelligence. Many books and web sites cover the topic of multiple intelligences. Pupils could look at the skills they have chosen and consider which intelligences are more developed.

★ Pupils could also consider which adult jobs their and other peoples' particular strengths might be suited to (e.g. footballer, hairdresser, lawyer, secretary, nurse, doctor, lorry driver, artist, plumber, architect, decorator, TV presenter, surgeon, teacher, shop assistant, traffic warden, writer, vet, tree surgeon, clothes designer, actor, car mechanic, estate agent, librarian, window cleaner, waiter/waitress, paramedic, running a business, builder, accountant, counsellor, carpenter, fire-fighter, athlete, receptionist, chef, computer programmer).

★ Pupils could interview each other about their strengths and give examples of how they know they have those strengths.

GETTING COMPLIMENTS (PAGE 11)

Purpose of activity: To consider the positive impact of compliments.

Key discussion points

★ Nearly everyone loves to receive compliments.

★ Some people give more compliments than others.

★ People can just decide that they are going to give more compliments to other people.

★ The great thing about compliments is that the more you give, the more you are likely to get.

★ When someone gives a person a compliment, some people shun it and refuse to believe or accept it. The best thing to do is say thank you and be pleased!

★ Jealousy or not being used to giving compliments can stop people from giving them.

Extension activities

★ Brainstorm 'nice things we could say about someone' and leave them displayed prominently.

★ Give pupils a sheet of blank A4 paper and ask them to write and decorate their name in the middle of the sheet leaving plenty of space around the outside. Next, explain to pupils that they must not look at the piece of paper again until you say so and that they are to leave the paper on the desk where they usually sit. Then ask pupils to wander around the classroom writing compliments on each others' sheets. Encourage children to write on everyone's sheet but stress that if pupils cannot think of a compliment then not to write anything as it would be distressing for someone to find something insulting written on their sheet. You (the teacher) can also write something on each of their sheets.

★ Pupils could make a compliments card for someone.

WHAT ARE YOU LIKE? (PAGE 12)
Purpose of activity: To reflect on personal qualities.
Key discussion points

★ We all have different personalities and different strengths.

★ It's a good idea to have an awareness of our strengths (and weaknesses) and how they affect other people. Knowing yourself is called intra-personal intelligence.

Extension activities

★ Pupils could invent the nastiest person in the world and describe his or her character using words like: selfish, rude, negative…etc. They could then discuss how people would react to him or her.

★ Pupils could anticipate how their parents/carers would mark them for each quality and then take the sheet home to find out the actual score they give them.

PUT THEM IN ORDER (PAGE 13)
Purpose of the activity: To explore preferences and values.
Key discussion points

★ Everyone has different preferences and values. The fact that we are all different makes the world an interesting place.

★ Reflecting on our own preferences and values helps us to become more self aware.

★ When anyone shows an interest in anything that is unique and personal to you, it can make you feel good!

Extension activities

★ Pupils could make up their own 'put them in order' challenges for other members of the class to complete. Pupils could also make up one for the teacher!

★ Pupils could discuss the following questions about the activity:
　　1. Which lists did you find hardest to order?
　　2. Did you surprise yourself with any of your answers?
　　3. Did you learn anything about yourself?

A ROOM OF YOUR OWN (PAGE 14)
Purpose of activity: To explore preferences.
Key discussion points

★ Four hours is long enough to get bored (if you had nothing to do) but not so long that you would need a great variety of entertainment. Pupils need to

basically imagine how each choice might enhance their time in the room and which things, therefore they would prefer.

★ Nearly everyone watches television. If pupils choose to have a television, you could question if they might like to use this as an opportunity to try something new.

★ The choice of person will need careful consideration as it would be awful to be stuck in a room with someone that irritated you!

Extension activities

★ Pupils could draw the view from their window.
★ Pupils could draw their choices and write about why they chose them.

WHAT GOALS CAN I SET MYSELF? (PAGE 15)

Purpose of the activity: To establish personal areas for development and set goals to make improvements.

Key discussion points

★ Some things we cannot change about ourselves, but many things we can, if we are determined to. Sometimes, all it takes is awareness of what needs improving!

★ Behaviour can be changed.

★ Setting yourself goals means that you have committed yourself to focusing on that particular issue with the hope of personal development.

Extension activities

★ Pupils can make challenge cards. They can set themselves three or more challenges and revisit the challenges every two weeks. They could give themselves a mark out of ten for how close to their goal they think they are and comment on any changes in the way they do things or anything that happened differently as a result of their new behaviour.

★ Pupil could set themselves lifetime goals! (e.g. learn to drive, get a job I enjoy, have children, be a good person, travel…etc)

DO YOU LIKE A CHALLENGE? (PAGE 16)

Purpose of activity: For pupils to think about the benefits of being determined to rise to challenges.

Key discussion points

★ Most people are scared of, or uncomfortable about, failing and everyone likes the feeling of success.

★ If a person can feel more positive about failing, they are more likely to be tenacious at whatever it is they are trying to do.

★ Failing needs to be accepted as a part of learning.

★ Many things cannot be learned instantly and need practice or a few attempts before a person can do them.

★ Some things, such as learning a new language or learning a musical instrument take a lot of time and determination before a person becomes competent – but the rewards are worth striving for.

★ Many skills become easier as our motor skills improve throughout childhood and into adulthood. There are many things that seem hard at first but nearly everyone learns to do as they grow up e.g. learn to tie shoe laces, tell the time, ride a bike, swim, write, read, cook, spell, throw and catch, use different tools, etc

★ No one can be good at everything all of the time!

Extension activities

★ Ask pupils to discuss the idea that people might give up really easily with some things but be more determined with others. This can depend on what a person considers himself or herself to be good at. e.g. someone who believes they are good at sport might always have a go at anything sporty but if they believe they are no good at art, they might give up really easily when they are asked to draw something.

★ Pupils could make up a cartoon showing how Determined Dan did not give up and eventually succeeded.

★ Pupils could draw a cartoon of themselves succeeding at a challenge they think is really difficult.

YOU ARE UNIQUE!

Complete this sheet.

1. Your full name is _____

2. If you could eat anything you wanted right now, what would it be?

_____

3. Draw a picture of a person's head in this box. Give them a hat to wear.

4. If you could be called a different name, what would you like it to be?

_____

5. What is your favourite lesson at school?

_____

6. If you had to be an animal, which animal would you be? _____

7. Which of the following activities do you like doing? (ring them)

singing   cycling   science experiments   drawing   shopping   reading stories

playing football   tidying your bedroom   doing jigsaw puzzles   cutting your toenails

8. Put the activities in order from the thing you would most like to do right now to the thing you would least like to do. Write the order of your letters here:

_____

    a) Go to a hot sunny beach   b) Go to the fair   c) Go to the cinema
d) Go to an art lesson   e) Play a game of rounders   f) Have a meal in a restaurant

9. If you were asked to give these pet monsters a name, what would you call each one?

    Name _____   Name _____   Name _____

10. Design a signature for yourself:

11. Design a wallpaper pattern on the back of this sheet using only circles, squares and triangles. Colour your design.

I BET YOU, NOBODY ELSE IN THE CLASS WILL HAVE FILLED IN THIS SHEET IN EXACTLY THE SAME WAY AS YOU HAVE!

WONDERFUL ME

1. My full name is _____ . I think I was given my name by

_____ . If I could be called another name, I would like it to be

_____ . My nickname is _____ (if you don't have

one, make one up that you'd like to have).

2. Some words that I would use to describe myself are (ring any you think could
be used):

tidy   kind   cheerful   sporty   fun   quiet   noisy   unusual   creative   practical

3. This is how I draw...

| a tree | a face | a dog | a flower |

I think the _____ is the best picture out of the four that I drew.

4. If all the walls in my house had to be painted one colour, I would choose: _____

5. If I had the choice of the following for my next meal, I would choose:

pizza   roast chicken   lasagne   egg and chips   a cheese sandwich

6. Something I really like about myself is: _____

7. Something I wish I could be better at is: _____

8. When I grow up, I would really like to be a: _____

9. At school, I think I am best at: (choose three)

    listening to instructions   playing   drawing   answering questions

helping others   playing sport   trying hard   finishing work   being neat

    following instructions   getting on with other people   abiding by the rules

        describing things   joining in   having ideas

10. Something I could never be without is: _____

PSHE AND CITIZENSHIP 7-9 © MOLLY POTTER 2008

YOUR STRENGTHS

Are you better at...

doing sums	or	remembering to use capital letters and full stops
drawing	or	writing
throwing a ball a long distance	or	catching a ball
remembering a poem off by heart	or	designing a new outfit
writing a story	or	telling a joke
juggling	or	tightrope walking
cooking	or	sewing
listening	or	talking
singing	or	acting
using a map	or	following directions
mending a puncture	or	painting a picture
doing a jigsaw puzzle	or	doing a crossword
giving instructions	or	following instructions
learning spellings	or	learning times tables
working in a team	or	working on your own
doing a science experiment	or	making a model of something
dancing	or	climbing a tree
making new friends	or	making up with people who you have fallen out with
speaking in assembly	or	organising a game for several people to play
playing a musical instrument	or	speaking another language
persuading someone to do something	or	sorting out arguments
understanding how other people feel	or	explaining how you feel
playing a computer game	or	getting information from a book
being able to change your plans at the last minute	or	being organised

Put a star by the 5 things on this sheet you think you are best at.

On the back of this sheet list five things you have done or five things you are good at doing that you are proud of.

Your five things could be your talents, something you have achieved, how you treat your friends or something people compliment you on.

PSHE AND CITIZENSHIP 7-9 © MOLLY POTTER 2008

Which of the following compliments would you most like to receive? Choose five.

You are kind.	You make me laugh.
I always enjoy being with you.	You are good at art.
You are good at sport.	You are good fun.
You are a cheerful person.	I like working with you.
I like your shoes.	You always cheer me up.
You are easy to talk to.	I like your new haircut.
You have a great imagination.	You are really helpful.
I like you.	You are interesting.
Seeing you always makes my day better.	I hope we will always be friends.
You are unusual.	You are good at maths.
You are generous.	You are good at writing.
Everyone likes you.	You are confident.

I. How does getting a compliment make you feel?

2. How does giving a compliment make you feel?

TALK ABOUT

3. If someone gives you a compliment, what do you think you should say?

4. Do you feel better when you get a compliment about how you look, about something you have done or about your personality?

5. Mark yourself on this line.

I give lots of compliments   **I don't give any compliments**

- -

6. What would be the best ever compliment you could get and who would you like to receive it from? Write your answer on the back of this sheet.

PSHE AND CITIZENSHIP 7-9 © MOLLY POTTER 2008

WHAT ARE YOU LIKE?

Mark yourself out of ten for each of the following qualities (I is the lowest and IO the highest). Fold over your column and then ask a friend to do the same for you. Finally, ask a second friend to do the same.

	A friend's mark out of ten	Another friend's mark out of ten	Your mark out of ten (fold this over once completed)
Careful			
Good at concentrating			
Good at sharing			
Calm			
Honest			
Confident			
Unusual			
Polite			
Good at remembering			
Imaginative			
Tidy			
Trustworthy			
Chatty			
Enthusiastic			
Good at saying nice things about people			
Willing to try new things			
Hardworking			
Not easily annoyed by other people			
A good listener			
Helpful			
Fun			
Friendly			
Good at coming up with new ideas			
Good at forgiving people			
Gentle			
Good at working in a group			
Interesting			
Lively			

What have you learnt about yourself? _____

_____

PSHE AND CITIZENSHIP 7-9 © MOLLY POTTER 2008

PUT THEM IN ORDER

Rank each list in order starting with 'the most' (number this 1) and finishing with 'the least' (number varies).

The things you like the most to the things you like the least:

☆ 1. maths   literacy   music   **PE**   art   history   science

☆ 2. summer   winter   autumn   spring

☆ 3. cats   dogs   rabbits   tigers   elephants   hamsters

The things you find the most difficult to the things you find least difficult:

☆ 1. maths   literacy   music   **PE**   art   history   science

☆ 2. tying shoelaces   doing handstands   learning tables   whistling

☆ 3. saying sorry   complimenting someone   making up with someone   comforting someone

The things you think are most important to the things you consider least important:

☆ 1. having friends   having a hobby you enjoy   learning things at school   having a home

☆ 2. being confident   being tidy   being happy   being good looking

☆ 3. having tasty food   having a comfortable sofa   having nice wallpaper   not being too cold

From the things that influence you (have an effect on you) the most to the least:

☆ 1. where you are   who you're with   the time of day   what people have said to you recently

☆ 2. **TV**   friends   adults at home   teachers

☆ 3. music   the weather   how busy you are   how tired you are

From the things that annoy you the most to those that annoy you the least:

☆ 1. a dripping tap   getting dirt on your clothes   a pencil that won't sharpen   a power cut in the middle of a **TV** programme

☆ 2. being late   forgetting to bring something   getting lost   losing something

☆ 3. people being bossy   people boasting   people talking over you   people not listening to you

NOW COMPARE YOUR SHEET WITH SOMEONE ELSE'S.

PSHE AND CITIZENSHIP 7-9 © MOLLY POTTER 2008

A ROOM OF YOUR OWN

You are going to spend four hours in a large room. This is a totally imaginary situation and it's just a way of exploring the things you like!

The room has all your basic needs taken care of. There is a tap with drinking water, a toilet, a chair, light from a window, and the room is a comfortable temperature.

You are allowed to choose a few additional things to keep you entertained and comfortable. What would you choose?

Things that could be put into the room beforehand (Choose 2)	★ a carpet ★ an armchair ★ a sofa ★ a bed ★ a table ★ a bath ★ a big cushion ★ a big fluffy rug 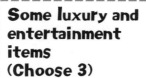
Some luxury and entertainment items (Choose 3)	★ a T.V. ★ a radio ★ a musical instrument ★ a mixture of art and craft materials ★ a telephone ★ a book of your choice ★ a meal of your choice ★ some tools and materials to make a kite ★ a basketball hoop and ball ★ a portable games console ★ a huge puzzle book – full of different types of puzzle ★ a dart board ★ an exercise machine ★ an ice cream machine with a choice of flavours and toppings ★ a board game of your choice 
Things that belong to you that are not in the other lists (Choose 4)	
One person	
The view from your window – what would you choose?	

PSHE AND CITIZENSHIP 7-9 © MOLLY POTTER 2008

WHAT GOALS CAN I SET MYSELF?

Consider the following statements and tick the box that best shows how you feel about each thing. If you think you are good at something but also think you could be better at it, tick both boxes.

	This is true about me	I could be better at this
HOW WELL I WORK AT SCHOOL		
I always try to concentrate hard in lessons.		
I enjoy a challenge and I'm not put off if I find something difficult.		
I nearly always finish my work.		
I listen well to instructions.		
I ask questions in class.		
I contribute to class discussions.		
If I don't understand how to do something, I always ask for help.		
I always try my best.		
HOW WELL I GET ON WITH OTHERS		
I'm good at sharing with other people.		
I have good manners.		
I understand that I can't always have everything my way.		
If I disagree with something someone says, I can argue calmly and respectfully.		
I'm good at making up with people I fall out with.		
I'm good at giving other people compliments.		
I work well in a team.		
I'm good at listening to what my friends say.		
I never moan about people behind their backs.		
I always talk worries through with people.		
PERSONAL STRENGTHS		
I'm good at explaining how I feel.		
I'm always ready to have a go at new things.		
I usually only need to be asked to do something once by the adults at home.		
I like helping other people.		
I hardly ever moan about things.		
I'm good at cheering people up if they're upset.		

Choose three things that you would like to be better at. (You don't need to just pick things from the list – if you can think of others, add them too.)

1. --

2. --

3. --

PSHE AND CITIZENSHIP 7-9 © MOLLY POTTER 2008

DO YOU LIKE A CHALLENGE?

Rank these things in order from the thing you find the least difficult (I) to the most difficult (9).

Colouring in neatly □

Doing a cartwheel □

Throwing a tennis ball a long way □

Learning spellings □

Learning times tables □

Skipping with a rope □

Batting in rounders □

Using capital letters in the right place □

Tying a bow □

Put a cross somewhere on these lines to show how much you agree or disagree with each sentence.

If I can't do something, I'll keep trying until I can do it.

Disagree --------------------------------- Agree

I feel great when I eventually learn how to do something that I once found difficult.

Disagree --------------------------------- Agree

I'm not scared of a challenge.

Disagree --------------------------------- Agree

Think of something...

you once found difficult but that you can now do.

you find difficult that you are determined to be able to do or get better at.

you gave up trying to learn or do.

you can't do and that you can't ever imagine being able to do.

DISCUSS

How do you think a person feels when they try to do something difficult?

How does a person feel when they succeed at doing something they once could not do?

What advice would you give to someone about facing a challenge?

PSHE AND CITIZENSHIP 7-9 © MOLLY POTTER 2008

A FOCUS ON RELATIONSHIPS

FRIENDSHIPS (PAGE 20)

Purpose of this activity: For pupils to have considered what they value in friendships.

Activity notes: Read through all of the cards at the beginning of the lesson and check for understanding. This activity is best done with pairs discussing each issue and jointly deciding which category it goes into.

Key discussion points

★ Different people value different things in friendships – which can mean that a person who will be a good friend to one person might not suit another!

★ Forgiveness can help to maintain friendships. Forgiveness allows people the opportunity to move on from their mistakes and we all make mistakes.

★ Some people appear to be more consistent than others but within any friendship, it is healthy to be able to accept that some people just have bad days and won't always be able to deliver what we might think we need from the friendship.

★ Nobody is perfect or good at absolutely everything. It is common to have different friends that we turn to for different things. We might turn to one friend to talk through something we are worried about and to another to have a laugh!

Extension activities

★ Pupils could write a list of sentence ends for the sentence, 'A good friend…'

★ Pupils could design and label an ideal friend.

WHAT DO YOU LOOK FOR IN A FRIEND? (PAGE 21)

Purpose of this activity: For pupils to have considered what they value in friendships.

Key discussion points

★ Different people value different things in friendships – which can mean that a person that will be a good friend to one person might not suit another!

★ Nobody is perfect or good at absolutely everything. It is common to have different friends that we turn to for different things. We might turn to one friend to talk through something we are worried about and to another to have a laugh!

★ Everyone makes mistakes – even in their friendships. It is healthy to be able to forgive people if they do something that upsets you – especially if they are sorry.

Extension activities

★ Pupils could complete the following sentence: what I would expect to have in a good friendship….

★ Pupils can think of all the things they give and get from a friendship.

★ Pupils could draw and label their ideal friend.

★ Pupils could consider what they like most about each of their friends.

★ Pupils could make an advert 'selling' the wonderfulness of having friends.

★ Pupils could stick the qualities onto an 'importance spectrum' - showing a progression on a scale from qualities they believe to be really important to not important at all.

GETTING ON WITH OTHER PEOPLE (PAGE 22)

Purpose of activity: To consider behaviour that helps a person to get on with others.

Key discussion points

★ Very few people get on with everyone all the time.

★ Certain behaviours help people to get along such as: being friendly, smiling, being helpful, listening, being honest (except for tactful white lies), being prepared to compromise, not gossiping, respecting other people and their property, being concerned about how other people feel and keeping promises.

Extension activities

★ Pupils could write and illustrate a guide to getting on with other people.

★ Pupils could consider gossiping and why it is an unpleasant thing to do.

A GOOD AND A BAD ENDING! (PAGE 23)

Purpose of the activity: To consider effective communication during potentially volatile situations.

Key discussion points

★ If people communicate effectively, misunderstandings and upset can be avoided.

★ Quite often the first few moments of any situation can influence what happens. If people remain calm, things are less likely to turn nasty.

★ Communicating effectively might include rules such as:
1. Listen to each other carefully
2. Try very hard to find out all the facts
3. Do not jump to conclusions
4. Try to avoid making accusations
5. Keep calm and try not to raise your voice

6. Do try not to insult the other person

7. Make sure you both get the chance to speak

8. Try to imagine how the other person feels and take their feelings into account.

9. If you are angry or upset, you might need to take time out to calm down before you make time to listen to the other person.

10. Give people the opportunity to say sorry and accept their apology.

Extension activities

★ Pupils could imagine a situation where two cars have crashed into each other (nobody is hurt) and consider what advice they would give to the two drivers so that no one ends up angry or upset. Does this advice need to change if one of the drivers quite clearly was to blame for the crash?

★ Pupils could consider which emotions can make us communicate less effectively!

SAYING SORRY (PAGE 24)

Purpose of activity: To consider why we apologise and how to do it well!

Key discussion points

★ Saying sorry is pointless unless we mean it.

★ To mean what we say, we need to fully understand and acknowledge how our actions hurt or upset another person.

★ If we hurt someone accidentally (with words or physically) we are apologising for causing the other person's hurt to show that we would never actually want it to happen.

★ A good apology is said 1) with understanding of what is being apologised for, 2) said looking the person in the eye, 3) said in a clear voice with a serious tone, and 4) said with the intention of whatever you are apologising for never happening again.

★ Sometimes apologising needs to be two-way.

★ Forgiveness is an important part of apologising. Forgiveness is the art of allowing other people to move on from their mistakes.

Extension activities

★ Pupils could write a letter from a problem page that is all about the need to say sorry. Pupils can also write the advice that responds to the letter.

★ Pupils could write guidance for 'how to say sorry properly'.

SORTING OUT CONFLICT (PAGE 25)

Purpose of activity: To consider effective conflict resolution.

Key discussion points

★ Some conflicts are not straightforward to solve after an event has happened. Lessons can be learned from conflicts about how to carry things out in future, e.g. with Maddy and Ash, they could agree that once something is swapped, that is it – for good.

★ Conflicts are rarely effectively resolved if people show anger during negotiations. People need an opportunity to calm down before they try to sort out the conflict.

★ Considering people's feelings can be a big part of conflict resolution. Encouraging people to empathise can diffuse anger.

★ Dealing with conflict is not about winning or losing, it is about negotiating a compromise that everyone can agree to.

PSHE AND CITIZENSHIP 7-9 © MOLLY POTTER 2008

Extension activities
★ Pupils could role-play Maddy and Ash arguing and then have a third person step in to mediate.

★ Pupils could write the golden rules of sorting out conflict.

★ Pupils could think of other examples of situations that can cause conflict and consider what compromises could be negotiated. (e.g. twins celebrating their birthday together – one wants a disco, the other wants to go ice skating but their parents won't let them do both).

AS THE STORY UNFOLDS (PAGE 26)
Purpose of the activity: To explore how a situation can escalate, how this escalation could be prevented and how best to make up after two people have fallen out.

Key discussion points
★ Quite often a misunderstanding causes a situation to escalate and further communication could usually prevent it. If Jaz had explained to Jackie that he had only been trying to entertain her by pulling a funny face, nothing more would have happened.

★ Both Jackie and Jaz played a part in letting the situation get so nasty.

★ Actually hitting someone is often considered to be more wrong than calling someone a name, but name calling is wrong and hurtful too.

★ Laughing at someone because they are upset is a nasty thing to do. If you realise that what you have done has upset someone, that is a good time to apologise! It is good to accept responsibility for what you have done, rather than laugh at another person's upset.

★ In order to apologise and mean it, Jackie and Jaz both need to take responsibility for what they did and empathise with the other person so they can understand how their behaviour made the other person feel. This involves a lot of effective (calm, good listening, equal etc.) communication – and a mediator might be needed.

★ Both Jackie and Jaz can learn from their mistakes and try not to let a situation like this happen again.

Extension activities
★ Pupils could draw a cartoon of another 'escalation' and then label it with advice saying what could have been done at key points to prevent the situation getting nastier and nastier.

★ Pupils could write the top ten tips for making up.

GOOD TO TALK (PAGE 27)
Purpose of the activity: To look at 'good' and 'bad' communication, and appreciate the effect it has on the person you are talking to.

Key discussion points
★ Some physical things (eye contact, nodding…etc.) can have a big impact on how well a conversation goes. When someone is really engaged in a conversation with another person, they often mirror the other person's movement and stance.

★ Anything that makes a person seem like they are not really listening (e.g. only talking about themselves, asking questions that show they have not listened or being dismissive) can ruin a conversation.

★ Good conversation skills can be practised.

★ If you are talking to someone and they don't make you feel listened to, it can be quite uncomfortable.

Extension activities
★ Pupils could write the top five tips for being a good person to talk to.

★ Pupils could draw and label Tina/Toby Talk – the best person to talk to in the world.

★ Pupils could write a list of conversation blockers. e.g. no eye contact, asking no questions, looking at your watch, sighing… etc.

KINDNESS (PAGE 28)
Purpose of activity: To consider kindness and how some acts of kindness are very easy to carry out.

Key discussion points
★ Kindness is the act of giving behaviour towards others. What a person gives can vary. It could be time, attention, a listening ear, money, helpfulness, warm-heartedness, a present, a card, positivity, encouragement, compliments, friendliness, a pleasant surprise etc.

★ It could be that the more effort that is made to be kind, the greater a person's kindness is as they have, in effect, given more. However, small acts of kindness do add up!

Extension activities
★ Pupils could construct a list of ten kind things a person could do.

★ Pupils could illustrate kindness and what they believe it means.

★ Pupils could make up the cartoon adventures of superhero Kaptain Kindness.

PSHE AND CITIZENSHIP 7-9 © MOLLY POTTER 2008

FRIENDSHIPS

I. In any friendship, how often would you expect to have each of the following?

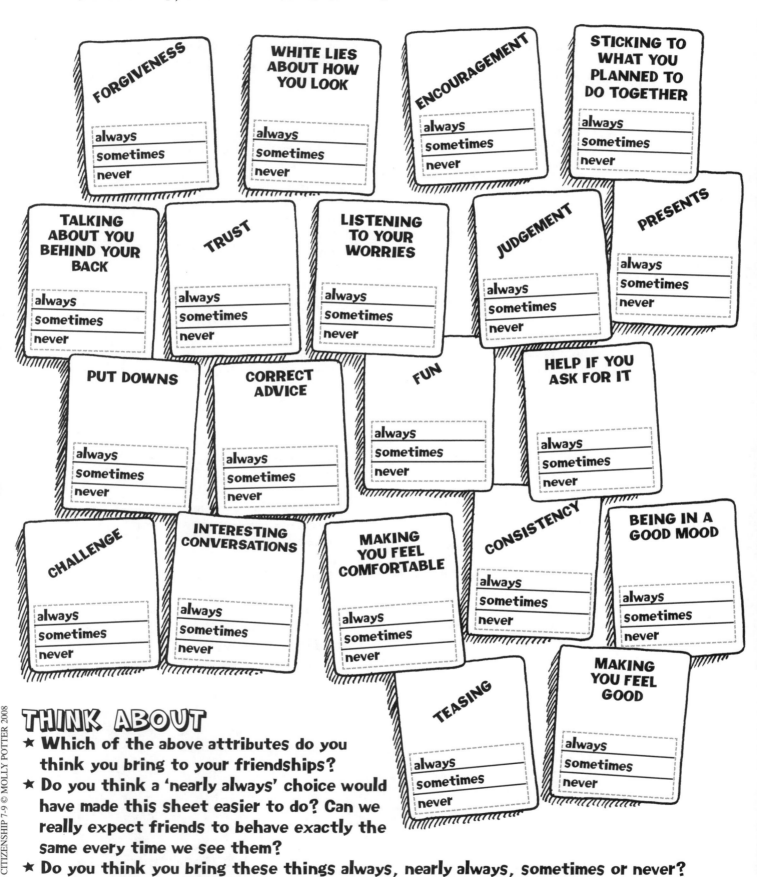

FORGIVENESS
- always
- sometimes
- never

WHITE LIES ABOUT HOW YOU LOOK
- always
- sometimes
- never

ENCOURAGEMENT
- always
- sometimes
- never

STICKING TO WHAT YOU PLANNED TO DO TOGETHER
- always
- sometimes
- never

TALKING ABOUT YOU BEHIND YOUR BACK
- always
- sometimes
- never

TRUST
- always
- sometimes
- never

LISTENING TO YOUR WORRIES
- always
- sometimes
- never

JUDGEMENT
- always
- sometimes
- never

PRESENTS
- always
- sometimes
- never

PUT DOWNS
- always
- sometimes
- never

CORRECT ADVICE
- always
- sometimes
- never

FUN
- always
- sometimes
- never

HELP IF YOU ASK FOR IT
- always
- sometimes
- never

CHALLENGE
- always
- sometimes
- never

INTERESTING CONVERSATIONS
- always
- sometimes
- never

MAKING YOU FEEL COMFORTABLE
- always
- sometimes
- never

CONSISTENCY
- always
- sometimes
- never

BEING IN A GOOD MOOD
- always
- sometimes
- never

TEASING
- always
- sometimes
- never

MAKING YOU FEEL GOOD
- always
- sometimes
- never

THINK ABOUT
★ **Which of the above attributes do you think you bring to your friendships?**
★ **Do you think a 'nearly always' choice would have made this sheet easier to do? Can we really expect friends to behave exactly the same every time we see them?**
★ **Do you think you bring these things always, nearly always, sometimes or never?**
★ **If you were to give someone suggestions about being a good friend, what would you say to them?**

WHAT DO YOU LOOK FOR IN A FRIEND?

Decide whether each of the following qualities is 'very', 'quite' or 'not important' when it comes to your friends.

QUALITIES I LOOK FOR	Very important	Quite important	Not important
never lies to me			
makes me laugh			
good looking			
helpful			
listens to me if I'm upset			
generous			
dresses smartly			
gives me compliments			
rich			
never moans about me behind my back			
likes doing the same things as me			
easy going			
a good listener			
never teases me			
reliable			
willing to share things			
interesting			
makes time for me			
lives near me			
forgives easily			
likes me – just as I am			
doesn't moan about things			
easy to talk to			
sticks up for me			
smiles a lot			
Always in a good mood			

The most important qualities in a friend for me are:

1) _____

2) _____

3) _____

PSHE AND CITIZENSHIP 7-9 © MOLLY POTTER 2008

GETTING ON WITH OTHER PEOPLE

Tick one answer to each of these questions. Be as honest as you can!

If a new person joined your class would you:
a) **Introduce yourself to them straight away?**
b) **Watch them from a distance before you decide whether or not to get to know them?**
c) **Not bother to get to know them because you already have friends?**

Do you smile at people:
a) All the time?
b) Only if someone smiles at you?
c) Hardly ever?

If someone dropped all their things on the floor in front of you, would you:
a) **Immediately help them to pick everything up?**
b) **Only help them if they are a friend of yours?**
c) **Walk past them and not help at all?**

If a friend of yours is upset about something that is happening at home:
a) Are you prepared to listen to them as much as they want you to?
b) Will you listen to them for a while but then become bored and avoid letting them talk to you?
c) Not listen to them at all?

If your gran invited you over for lunch, and then someone invited you to a party on the same day you were going for lunch.
a) **Would you be honest and tell your gran that you had another offer and you really don't want to miss it?**
b) **Would you lie to your gran to get out of the party?**
c) **Would you just go ice skating and not say anything to your gran?**

If you wanted to go to the fair and your friend wanted to go to the cinema to see a film that was only showing once:
a) Would you be able to compromise and go to the cinema today and the fair tomorrow?
b) Would you go to the fair with another friend?
c) Would you argue and fall out?

Do you gossip about people you know:
a) **Never?**
b) **Sometimes?**
c) **All the time?**

Do you keep your promises:
a) Always?
b) It depends on whom you made the promise to?
c) Hardly ever?

If someone got upset because of something you said, even though you didn't mean to be nasty, would you:
a) **Say sorry and mean it?**
b) **Say sorry but not really mean it?**
c) **Laugh at them for getting upset?**

If someone lent you his or her new pen and you accidentally broke it would you:
a) Buy them a new one?
b) Hand it back and say sorry?
c) Say you lost it?

Look at your answers. Do you think you have lots of qualities that mean you can get on with other people?

On the back of this sheet list the qualities that a person usually has if other people find them easy to get on with.

PSHE AND CITIZENSHIP 7-9 © MOLLY POTTER 2008

Work with a partner and act out the following two scenarios with...

I. a bad ending (the worst possible ending leaving both people upset or angry)

2. a good ending (an ending where both people are happy)

SCENARIO 1 - THE MISUNDERSTANDING

Person A: You really like your friend's pencil case, so much in fact, that you go to town and buy one exactly the same.

Person B: Your pencil case has gone missing and you know that your friend always wanted one like yours.

Person A turns up with the new pencil case and sits next to Person B. What happens next?

SCENARIO 2 - A BAD START TO THE DAY

Person A: You have just been given a new bike and you're a bit embarrassed because you haven't quite mastered how to ride it. You wobble around and can only just manage to reach the ground.

Person B: Your mum told you off this morning, which put you in a bad mood. You left for school late and you have just realised that you've forgotten your packed lunch.

Person A knocks Person B over. What happens next?

Talk about the following questions for each scenario:
* ★ How did the bad endings make you feel?
* ★ What happened differently at the start of the good ending and the start of the bad ending?
* ★ What other differences did you notice between the scenario with the good ending and the one with the bad ending?

List some guidelines that would help the people in these scenarios. In other words, what is it important to do and not to do in situations like these?

PSHE AND CITIZENSHIP 7-9 © MOLLY POTTER 2008

SAYING SORRY

1. DO YOU THINK ALL OF THE FOLLOWING PEOPLE NEED TO SAY SORRY?

★ Janis accidentally tripped Frankie up because her foot was sticking out from under the desk.

★ Tracey forgot Greg's birthday – even though he was one of her best friends.

★ Harry got Peter into trouble because he lied and said that Peter had made a mess with the paints – when he hadn't.

★ Kate punched Mehmet at playtime because he called her stupid.

2. WHICH OF THE FOLLOWING DO YOU THINK ARE TRUE ABOUT SAYING SORRY?

	True	False
Saying sorry is just about using the word, 'sorry'.		
If you say sorry and mean it, you truly hope you won't repeat what you did.		
Saying sorry doesn't work if you say it in a grumpy voice.		
When you say sorry, you should be clear about what it is exactly, that you are saying sorry for.		
You don't really need to say sorry to someone if they get hurt because of an accident you caused – after all, it was an accident!		
If something you say upsets someone without you meaning to, it's still a good idea to say sorry.		

3. THE WORLD'S BEST AND THE WORLD'S WORST APOLOGY

Person A and Person B are in a technology lesson. They have spent many weeks building model castles and they are all very pleased with them. Person A lifts his/her castle up and carries it across the classroom but he/she trips and his/her castle lands right on top of Person B's castle. Both castles rip and wet paint from one smudges on to the other. Lots of the detail they spent so long putting on to their models has been destroyed.

A APOLOGISES TO B.
Role play the 'world's worst apology' then role play the 'world's best apology'.

Ash and Maddy collect toy trolls. They would do anything to get a new one to add to their collections. Sometimes they swap trolls. Last week, they did just that. Maddy swapped her pink-haired troll for a green-haired troll. At first they were both happy with this but now Maddy is saying she wants her old troll back. Ash says that he doesn't want to swap them back.

They have fallen out with each other and are arguing about the trolls. Normally, they are really good friends but this conflict means that they can't talk to each without getting angry or upset.

You are friends with Ash and Maddy and they have asked you to help them sort out their problem. Discuss what you think needs to happen.

Here are some pieces of advice people have offered for sorting out the conflict:

"Try to listen carefully and talk calmly – the moment someone loses their temper, nothing is likely to get resolved."

"Consider how you are both feeling. Both people in the conflict need to feel better."

"You need to find a way forward that both people will agree to. To do this you need to talk and also listen to each other."

"Try not to say anything nasty about the person you are in conflict with – that won't help anyone."

"If you do lose your temper, explain that you need to take time out to cool down."

PSHE AND CITIZENSHIP 7-9 © MOLLY POTTER 2008

Jackie kicked Jaz in the shin. The teacher saw it and told Jackie off. But that wasn't the whole story, let's go back in time....

It started when Jaz pulled a silly face at Jackie

This made Jackie pull a nasty face back at Jaz.

Jaz then called Jackie stupid.

This made Jackie very upset and she began sulking.

Jaz laughed at Jackie for sulking.

So Jackie kicked Jaz.

I. Now decide whether the following are true or false?

	TRUE	FALSE
Because Jaz started it, he should say sorry as he is to blame.		
Because Jackie actually kicked Jaz, she should say sorry because she physically hurt Jaz.		
Both Jackie and Jaz were responsible for what happened.		

2. When the teacher asked both Jackie and Jaz what had happened, this is what they both said.

If you were the teacher, what would you do with Jackie and Jaz after they had both given their side of the story?

(Remember, when two people fall out, the best thing that can happen is that they make up with each other properly.)

She kicked me. All I did was try to make her laugh by pulling a funny face and she kicked me.

Jaz

He called me stupid and laughed at me when I got upset.

Jackie

PSHE AND CITIZENSHIP 7-9 © MOLLY POTTER 2008

GOOD TO TALK

Which of the following do you think would make someone want to talk to you and which do you think would put them off? Cut each box out and sort them into two groups: 'bad for talking' and 'good for talking'.

Making eye contact

Looking at the clock or watch

Nodding and smiling

Yawning

Asking questions that show you are interested

Looking bored

Interrupting

Asking a question if you haven't understood what someone was saying

Mumbling

Making sure both people get a chance to talk

ROLE-PLAY

Work with a partner. Imagine a new person has joined your class.

Act out a scene where you first meet this new person in the playground.

On the first occasion, be someone who the new pupil won't bother talking to again because you are showing many of the signs you put in the 'bad for talking' group.

On the second occasion, be someone who is great to talk to because you are showing many of the signs you put in the 'good for talking' group.

PSHE AND CITIZENSHIP 7-9 © MOLLY POTTER 2008

KINDNESS

Work with a partner and talk about the following questions:

1. What do you think kindness is? _____

_____

_____

_____

2. Rank the following acts of kindness in order from the most easy to do (1) to the most difficult (8).

| Sharing your things | | Smiling | |

| Listening to someone who is upset | | Saying 'hello' to welcome someone | |

| Forgiving someone who has been nasty to you | | Letting someone you don't normally play with join in with your game | |

| Opening the door for someone | | Helping someone if they get stuck with their work | |

3. When someone is kind to you, how does that make you feel?

_____

_____

_____

4. If your school was to write a 'Kindness Policy', what kind of things do you think it would include?

_____

_____

_____

PSHE AND CITIZENSHIP 7-9 © MOLLY POTTER 2008

EXPLORING ATTITUDES, OPINIONS AND VALUES

CHANGING OPINIONS (PAGE 32)

Purpose of activity: To explore how opinions can change when you find out more facts about a topic.

Key discussion points

★ When people discuss an issue, they can often change their opinion as they uncover more facts about it.

★ If King Jonas put his side of the story to you, you would probably think badly of the Harvellians. If the Harvellians told you their story they would probably make you think King Jonas was bad. This is because both King Jonas and the Harvellians would leave out the facts that might make you sympathetic to the other side of the argument.

★ The best way to consider your own opinion about any issue is to try and find out all the facts you can about any situation or issue, think about it carefully (possibly discuss it) and then form an opinion.

Extension activities

★ Pupils could write the Harvellians' version of the story – how they would tell it and King Jonas' version of the story – how he would tell it. Both 'sides' would leave out any facts that made you support the other side of the argument. They might also make persuasive comments or exaggerate things – for example King Jonas might exaggerate about the crime the Harvellian woman committed.

★ Pupils could work in pairs to develop their own story that could change people's opinions as it unfolded.

NASTY NORBERT (PAGE 33)

Purpose of this activity: For pupils to consider the effect of different personality traits and which they most value in a person.

Activity notes

Pupils will probably need to be given meanings of some of the negative and positive personality traits listed on the sheet.

Key discussion points

★ Pupils can consider which qualities will have the most impact on improving Norbert's behaviour and make him a more pleasant person to have as a son.

★ Pupils will find that they value some qualities far more than others.

Extension activities

★ Pupils could role-play the new Norbert demonstrating his new qualities.

★ Pupils could value each of the qualities - out of ten - for importance.

★ Pupils could consider which of the negative personality traits that Norbert demonstrated that they like the least.

GET RID OF THREE (PAGE 34)

Purpose of activity: To explore perceptions of what causes most sadness, discomfort or difficulty in a person's life.

Key discussion points

★ Some of these things can sometimes be beneficial at times– such as making mistakes (we learn from this), being scared (can make us avoid danger) and being told what to do (sometimes we need guidance).

★ It is sometimes the negative things in life that teach us most.

★ Negative things can make us really appreciate the good times in our lives.

Extension activities

★ Pupils could order the things on the page from most negative to least negative.

★ Pupils can consider what they could actually do (if anything) to minimise the chances of the three things they chose happening in their life. e.g. illness – balanced diet, exercise or getting irritated by other people – trying hard to focus on the good things about people and forgiving them for their weaknesses!

BOYS AND GIRLS (PAGE 35)

Purpose of activity: To challenge sexual stereotyping.

Key discussion points

★ A 'non-conforming' boy is more likely to be teased than a 'non-conforming' girl.

★ Traditionally girls/women are 'meant to' be clean, be neat, be sensitive, be responsible, be able to show different emotions, be good at looking after things, be gentle, be helpful and well behaved, like pink and like lessons such as sewing, cooking and art.

★ Traditionally boys/men are 'meant to' be energetic, be good at sport, not show emotion unless it's anger, hate pink, be strong, be prepared to get messy, like doing rather than talking and like lessons that involve fixing things or science.

★ Sexual stereotyping can cause people to be picked on for being, or being perceived as, different. Difference needs to be celebrated.

★ It usually takes courage not to conform and be different.

Extension activities:

★ Girls and boys could bring in their favourite toys. Everyone could write down the toy they would most like to play with and the toy they would least like to play with. Pupils could then look at the toy they like and then have a go at playing with the toy they stated they would least like to play with. This usually means that both genders will have tried out toys that are traditionally aimed at the opposite sex. Pupils could feedback what this felt like.

★ The pupils could consider careers that are frequently gender stereotyped such as fire-fighter, police, nurses, doctors, dentists, builders…etc

★ Pupils could challenge sexual stereotyping with posters saying things like it's OK to like pink whether you are a girl or a boy, it's very prejudiced to think that all fire-fighters will be men, boys should cry and tell you what they are feeling etc.

SIMILARITIES AND DIFFERENCES (PAGE 36)

Purpose of activity: To acknowledge that people have many similarities but also have many ways in which they can vary.

Key discussion points:

★ All humans have basic needs (e.g. sleep) and nearly all share some preferences (e.g. not being insulted).

★ Having your basic needs met is often considered a right. As basic needs are common to all people, it is considered to be a right that a person receives them.

★ Differences can be physical, related to our capabilities, about preferences, or about beliefs,

attitudes and values. The fact that we have many differences makes the world an interesting place.

Extension activities:

★ Pupils can work in pairs to discover many details about each other. They can then write a list of as many similarities and differences as they can find with each other.

★ Pupils can make posters showing what everyone likes (and needs). For example, praise, friends, achievement etc…

THREE GIFTS (PAGE 37)

Purpose of activity: To consider which skills pupils value.

Key discussion points:

★ Pupils could consider how the skills they have chosen would impact on their lives.

★ Pupils could debate which skills they think are things everyone could acquire (if they were determined enough) and which skills they think a person is born with.

Extension activities:

★ Pupils could list skills that they have already acquired.

★ Pupils could consider all the skills on the sheet and which jobs would suit them if they had each skill.

WHAT MAKES SOMETHING WRONG? (PAGE 38)

Purpose of activity: To reflect upon what makes something 'wrong'.

Key discussion points:

★ It is generally agreed that something is wrong if it harms or upsets another person deliberately or if it damages property.

★ Anything that deliberately puts yourself or other people at unnecessary risk from harm is also considered to be wrong.

★ Telling a lie can range from a small white lie (I like your new shoes) to a lie that could put someone in danger (a lie about where someone is). Other lies might just make a situation unfair (e.g. telling a lie to get out of PE). Telling a lie to avoid being told off is understandable but this is generally considered bad because if you do not admit to your wrongdoing, you have not taken responsibility for it and therefore are unlikely to change your ways!

Extension activities:

★ Pupils could illustrate a lie scale from not wrong (white) lies to seriously wrong and put their examples onto the scale.

★ Pupils could consider a series of 'crimes' (e.g. hitting, being rude) and what would be the best way to prevent a person from re-offending!

MAKING MISTAKES (PAGE 39)

Purpose of activity: To consider making mistakes, how everyone makes them and what can be done about them.

Key discussion points:

★ Everyone makes mistakes. A 'big' mistake might be one where someone ended up hurt or in danger, a small one might just leave someone a bit embarrassed or disappointed.

★ There are lots of reasons why people are scared to make mistakes - they don't want to look silly, everyone gets praised when they do things correctly but not if they do them incorrectly, they don't want to let other people down or they just don't like getting things wrong.

★ Sometimes good things come out of making mistakes e.g. better communication, learning something, forgiveness.

★ Some mistakes are accidents and some are done through carelessness or inconsideration. People find accidental mistakes easier to forgive than mistakes that are made through 'poor' judgement. People also tend to find mistakes that are repeated harder to forgive. (e.g. if a person kept missing an arrangement you had made with them).

★ The ways of dealing with mistakes depends on what the mistake was. You might communicate honestly and openly, say sorry and mean it, learn from the mistake and reduce the risk of it happening again or be determined to get it right next time.

★ People learn more effectively if they are not really scared of making mistakes.

Extension activities:

★ Pupils could consider how people could be made to feel better about making mistakes with school work.

★ Pupils could draw a cartoon of what they believe would be the best outcome for one of the mistakes on the sheet.

★ Pupils could think of another example for each of the following types of mistake and discuss what could be done about each mistake.
   1. Upsetting someone
   2. Causing an accident
   3. Putting someone in unnecessary danger
   4. Damaging something
   5. Being unable to do something you wanted to do
   6. Letting someone down
   7. Getting school work wrong

DIFFERENT POINTS OF VIEW (PAGE 40)

Purpose of the activity: To consider that it is OK for people to have different opinions and that opinions can change.

Key discussion points:

★ Most people have some issues that they have strong opinions about. Most people also have issues they have no or little opinion about. Opinions tend to develop as a person learns more about an issue or as they discuss it.

★ It is difficult to have a well-considered opinion about something you know little about.

★ Opinions can be swayed by how any issue is presented.

★ It is fine for people to have different opinions, as long as those opinions do not impact on the rights of others (e.g. racist views)

★ Preferences are not usually easily changed.

Extension activities:

★ Pupils could choose one of the issues on the sheet to debate. They could find out facts about the issue and decide how each fact could sway a person's opinion.

★ Pupils could consider the idea that it is OK to make personal choices that suit you as an individual (e.g. being a vegetarian) but to impose that on others would be denying individual choice.

CHANGING OPINIONS

An opinion is what you believe about something based on what you know.

Opinions can change, facts cannot.

Read the following story and after each section, write what you think of King Jonas in the second column of the table and in the third column what fact it was that made you think this.

	What is your opinion of King Jonas now?	What facts made you change your opinion? – if you did.
King Jonas ruled the island of Gorgolio and most of his subjects thought he was a kind and fair king. He was a cheerful man who liked to laugh and throw big parties for his subjects.		
In the far west of the island there was a small village called Harvelli. King Jonas treated the people that lived there (the Harvellians) quite differently from everyone else in his kingdom. He wouldn't let anyone leave the village and he wouldn't let anyone visit the people that lived there. They were treated like prisoners.		
King Jonas kept the Harvellians separate from the rest of the people in his kingdom simply because they were three times as big as anyone else on the island. He told people that it would be far safer if the two different sized people were kept apart.		
The Harvellians were convinced that King Jonas kept them trapped in their village because he was scared that they would take over the whole island and stop him from being king. The Harvellians insisted that they have no such plans and that they just wanted their freedom. Being trapped in their village made them very sad.		
King Jonas did not want to keep the Harvellians as prisoners but when he had first become king, they were allowed to roam all over the island. During this time, many of the smaller inhabitants had been injured or killed. At one point, a giant Harvellian woman was arrested for deliberately stamping on sheep. The Harvellians were adamant that the woman hadn't done anything wrong and that too much fuss was being made over a few dead sheep.		

PSHE AND CITIZENSHIP 7-9 © MOLLY POTTER 2008

NASTY NORBERT

Norbert, who was ten years old, was as nasty as a person can be to anyone and everyone! He was rude, mean, pathetic, whiny, dishonest, clumsy, spiteful, impatient, pessimistic, argumentative, selfish, insulting, grumpy, lazy, aggressive, sulky, ungrateful, greedy and unreliable. In fact, the only nice thing a person once managed to say about him was that his T-shirt was a nice colour.

Norbert had started this particular Saturday with a pretty foul argument with his mother over how much ice cream he should be allowed to eat for breakfast. He could never understand why his mum wouldn't let him eat the whole tub. So, as usual, he stormed out of the house without saying goodbye, slammed the door behind him and stomped off to the woods to see if he could find some stones to throw at the birds.

He found himself a tree stump to sit on so that he could have a good long sulk. As he was picking at a scab on his knee, he suddenly felt a hand on his shoulder and heard a gruff voice say,

'Ah there you are, I've been looking all over for you.'

Norbert turned round to set eyes upon something he'd never seen in his life, a sort of pixie with a large bag over his shoulder, a really long beard and a very stern look on his face. He was wearing a green tunic with a black belt around his waist – just like the pixies you see in fairy tales.

'What do you want?' snarled Norbert without the slightest hint of curiosity or interest. The pixie sat himself down next to Norbert on the tree stump and started to explain,

'I've been sent, along with my magic, to sort you out and to make your mother's life easier. You see I can do three magic spells, only three mind, and that's where I have to do some serious thinking. With each spell I can make one change. The idea is that I choose the three qualities that will have the biggest effect – I mean the three qualities that together will have the most chance of turning you into a nearly nice person!'

List the qualities you think the pixie should give on the back of this sheet, and explain why.

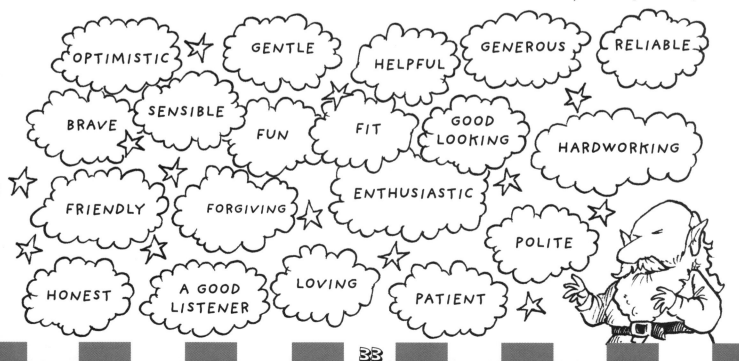

OPTIMISTIC GENTLE HELPFUL GENEROUS RELIABLE
BRAVE SENSIBLE FUN FIT GOOD LOOKING HARDWORKING
FRIENDLY FORGIVING ENTHUSIASTIC POLITE
HONEST A GOOD LISTENER LOVING PATIENT

PSHE AND CITIZENSHIP 7-9 © MOLLY POTTER 2008

GET RID OF THREE

If you could 'dispose' of three of the following, for the rest of your life, which would you choose?

| being told what to do | being scared | making mistakes |

| being tired when you're awake | being insulted — *you're stupid!* | being bored |

| worrying about what others think about you | regretting things you have done — *OOOPS!* | being ill |

| being lonely | finding something difficult to do | getting irritated by other people |

When you have chosen your three things – discuss these questions with a partner.
1) In what ways do you think not having these things would make your life better?
2) Is there anything else you would like to be able to dispose of?
3) Do you think any of the things on this page would be worth having in your life and if so, why?

Some people have quite an old fashioned view of what they think girls should do and what boys should do. Let's see what you think. Read the character descriptions below and then answer the questions at the end.

OLLIE AT 9

At school, Ollie loved art and cookery lessons. In the playground he mostly played with girls and liked to talk about the books that he'd read. He had lots of books and he took great care of them. Sometimes Ollie used to get upset at break times but when this happened he could usually talk to his friend, Katy, who always managed to cheer him up.

At home, Ollie loved looking after his pet guinea pig. He liked playing with dolls although he knew he could never tell the boys at school this.

OLLIE AT 20

Ollie works as a dancer. In his spare time he likes making clothes, cooking and going out to dinner with his girl-friend. He loves the colour pink and often makes and wears pink clothes.

CHARLOTTE AT 9

At school Charlotte loved football – in the playground or during games lessons. Charlotte often lost her temper and could get quite cross during some matches. In class, Charlotte was very untidy and hated the teacher always telling her about her handwriting being messy.

At home, Charlotte spent a lot of time sorting out her football stickers and watching football on the TV. She also liked fixing things and making model aeroplanes. Charlotte didn't have a favourite colour.

CHARLOTTE AT 20

Charlotte works as a lorry driver. In her spare time, she still likes to watch football with her boyfriend, Tim. She also has a black belt in karate. Charlotte loves D.I.Y. and has put a new kitchen into the house she bought about a year ago.

TALK ABOUT

★ What did you think of Ollie and Charlotte when you read about them? Be honest!
★ Have Ollie and Charlotte done anything wrong?
★ Do you think there are things a girl should never do or like?
★ Do you think there are things a boy should never do or like?

PSHE AND CITIZENSHIP 7-9 © MOLLY POTTER 2008

SIMILARITIES AND DIFFERENCES

Which of the following could you say are true of nearly everyone in your school and which are not.

	True of everyone in your school	Not true of everyone in your school
Purple is their favourite colour		
Needs to drink		
Likes maths best out of all the lessons		
Can smile		
Likes to receive a compliment		
Loves to play netball		
Loves eating brussel sprouts		
Needs to eat		
Would rather lie on a sunny beach than go to a fair		
Hates to be ignored		
Has blue eyes		
Likes to receive praise for doing good work		
Is scared of the dark		
Likes to be listened to		
Has long hair		
Likes to be treated fairly		
Likes to have friends		
Likes to feel safe		
Likes dogs		
Needs to sleep		
Likes to be respected and feel valued		
Doesn't like to be insulted		
Needs a home		

Give some examples of things all children in your class need, like or do.

Give some examples of the ways in which people can be different.

PSHE AND CITIZENSHIP 7-9 © MOLLY POTTER 2008

THREE 'GIFTS'

If you could choose three 'gifts' that would last for the rest of your life, which would you choose?

to be really good at remembering things

to be able to do really difficult sums in your head

to be a brilliant at drawing and painting

to be really good at fixing things

to be a brilliant dancer

to be able to make people laugh

to be great at making friends

to be able to speak another language

to be able to write really imaginative stories

to be able to play a musical instrument really well

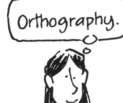
to be really good at spelling

to be a really fast runner

to be really good at explaining things

to be a really good singer

to be brilliant at using computers

to be really good at acting

to be really good at swimming

to be really good at science

NOW TALK ABOUT

1) If you had these gifts, how do you think you would use them in the rest of your life?

2) Is it better to be really good at one thing or quite good at lots of things?

3) How does being good at something make you feel?

PSHE AND CITIZENSHIP 7-9 © MOLLY POTTER 2008

WHAT MAKES SOMETHING WRONG?

What makes the following things wrong?

stealing

running across the road without looking

bullying

hitting someone

pushing into a queue

being rude to someone

deliberately breaking something that isn't yours

daring someone to do something dangerous

Decide which of the above are the most wrong – choose three.

1. _____

2. _____

3. _____

What about telling lies? Think of three different lies someone might tell. Are some more wrong than others?

_____

_____

_____

_____

_____

_____

MAKING MISTAKES

Do you think there is anyone in this world that has **NEVER** made a mistake? Which of the following mistakes do you think would be the hardest to sort out?

You forgot your **PE** kit and you have **PE** today.

You accidentally gave a party invitation to someone you didn't like.

You forgot that you left a pan of milk heating up on the cooker.

You spilt paint all over your friend's painting.

You were meant to meet you friend in the park at 10 a.m. but you turned up at 11 a.m.

You got all your work wrong in a science lesson

You told someone a secret about your friend and your friend found out.

You bought your friend a cake for her birthday that had nuts in and she is allergic to nuts.

DISCUSS

1. What would you do to try and sort out each of the mistakes?

2. What good things can sometimes happen because of mistakes?

3. What makes people scared of making mistakes?

4. Work in a group of at least three. Make up a freeze frame called 'the mistake'. Consider what would be the best thing to do after the mistake has happened.

PSHE AND CITIZENSHIP 7-9 © MOLLY POTTER 2008

DIFFERENT POINTS OF VIEW

Samia and Gregory were asked their opinions about some different topics.

Questions	Samia thinks...	Gregory thinks...
Which is the nicest colour to look at?	I think purple is the best colour.	Green – definitely.
Which is the most enjoyable lesson?	I like science best.	Art is the best lesson at school.
Which lesson at school is most important?	I think PE is the most important lesson because exercise keeps us healthy.	I think literacy because everyone needs to learn to read and write.
Are wet or outdoor breaks better?	Wet breaks	Outdoor breaks
What is it important for your friends to be like?	It's important that friends make you laugh.	I think it's important that you can trust your friends.
What do you think about school uniform?	A school uniform is a good idea because you don't have to think about what to wear each morning.	A school uniform is a bad idea because it makes everyone look the same.
Do you think you will ever be a vegetarian?	I am pretty sure that I will never be a vegetarian because I love meat.	I will always be a vegetarian.
What do you think about organic food?	I don't really know about organic food.	I think organic food is better for you.

DISCUSS

1) For each of the questions tick the opinion that you agree with most.

2) Do you think it matters that Samia and Gregory don't agree about these things?

3) If Samia and Gregory were to discuss these topics, do you think they might change their opinions about any of them?

4) What can make people change their point of view?

PSHE AND CITIZENSHIP 7-9 © MOLLY POTTER 2008

HEALTH AND SAFETY ISSUES

RISKY RITA AND NO-RISK RICK (PAGE 44)
Purpose of the activity: To consider taking appropriate risks and the fact you sometimes need confidence to take them.

Key discussion points:
★ If we were to never take any risks, our lives would be rather dull.

★ We need to take some risk in order to learn or to try new things.

★ The fear of the possibility of people laughing at us, people being nasty to us, of not liking something, or failure can prevent us from taking risks if we don't feel confident.

★ A risk can be a tiny leap into the unknown. Bigger leaps can take more confidence.

★ Sometimes people have to push themselves to take a risk, but they nearly always end up pleased that they did. This is because it means they have tried something new or slightly daring (like being in a school play) which is always exciting and can give you a thrill and a sense of achievement.

★ The risks covered in this activity are not risks that put someone in unnecessary danger – such risks are always considered foolish.

Extension activities:
★ Pupils could discuss what stops some people from taking risks and what the benefits of taking some risks can be.

★ Pupils could make up a new day for Rick – where he becomes Risky Rick.

WHEN DO YOU THINK IT WOULD BE SAFE? (PAGE 45)
Purpose of activity: To consider how everyone becomes more equipped and competent to keep themselves safe as they get older.

Key discussion points:
★ With babies (up to about 2 or 3) there is always a danger of choking if they play with small objects.

★ When children are very young (usually about 3 and under), they do not have the knowledge, competence or coordination to keep themselves safe with such things as scissors, slides, the bath, a pond and medicine.

★ With older children (8 upwards), their motor skills have improved and they can carry out more tasks if they have been taught how to safely.

★ The age at which it is commonly deemed that children can be out and about with no supervising adult is around 9. Again, it is wise that these children are equipped with knowledge about keeping themselves safe.

★ One of things in the table has a legal age limit: driving (17). This means that the age at which it is deemed appropriate has been well considered. The legal age for buying fireworks is 18; consequently it is probably considered that children should not light fireworks.

★ Although there is no age at which it is considered illegal to leave a child alone at home it is usually recommended that children under 13 are not left alone for very long.

★ Babysitting is quite a responsibility – therefore the age at which someone is left in charge of younger children is more about how responsible they are than anything!

Extension activities:
★ Pupils could consider what a child needs to be aware of to make tea, make toast, use a sharp knife, and keep safe.

★ Pupils could list all the rules at home and at school that are about keeping everyone safe.

★ Pupils could list a code of conduct for keeping themselves safe either a) when they are out and about (letting someone know where they are, being with another person, knowing dangerous adults exist though they are rare and how to get away from one, not going anywhere they don't know) or b) if they were ever left at home alone (knowing when to ring 999, being able to turn the gas or electricity off, having a trusted adult available that could be contacted, not letting strangers into the house etc.)

★ Pupils could consider the issue of independence – what it means, how it develops as a person grows up and how it is considered to be a good thing.

DANGER DETECTIVE (PAGE 46)
Purpose of activity: To consider potential dangers and how to minimise the risk of harm.

Key discussion points
★ There is no such thing as a life free from the risk of danger.

★ Measures can always be made to reduce the chances of a person being harmed e.g. with taking medicine, you only ever take medicine that has been prescribed for you and you follow the instructions on how to take it.

Extension activities
★ Pupils could consider the reasons why a person might not take obvious safety precautions such as wearing a seat belt (laziness, they don't care about themselves, they are rebelling, they are forgetful, they are not in the habit of using a seat belt).

★ Pupils could search for safety statistics from a variety of sources e.g. the internet, books, leaflets.

SNAZZ UP ROAD SAFETY (PAGE 47)
Purpose of activity: To revise road safety.

Key discussion points
★ Children aged eight have usually got a good understanding of road sense.

★ Parents/carers start to let children journey more independently at this age, therefore a revision of road safety is a good idea.

Extension activities
★ Pupils could design a sticker for young children to remind them of road safety rules.

★ Pupils could make a TV advert that gives an important road safety message to young children.

★ Pupils could take their ideas to test them out on younger children.

A MANUAL FOR MY BODY (PAGE 48)
Purpose of activity: To consider what maintains a healthy body.

Key discussion points:
★ A healthy lifestyle includes: not eating too many sugary, fatty or salty foods, eating plenty of fruit and vegetables, getting enough sleep, exercising (30 minutes a day), drinking plenty of fluid and keeping a healthy mind through not letting worries build up.

★ Obviously, a healthy mind is a complex issue and a full consideration would involve more than just thinking about the points included on the sheet. Mental health needs to be considered as important as physical health and should not be overlooked. There are many different factors that contribute to an individual's resilience.

Extension activities
★ Pupils could draw a body and label it with the words from the manual.

★ Pupils could consider what a very unhealthy lifestyle would look like and what the long-term risks of this would be.

FOLLIP AND FULLOP (PAGE 49)
Purpose of activity: To explore what a healthy lifestyle is with respect to eating and exercise.

Key discussion points
★ Follip and Fullop do absolutely no exercise. This is not at all healthy. They need to try and get more exercise into their day. There are lots of things pupils could suggest they do (e.g. walk to each others' houses when they visit, buy a bicycle and cycle to the shops, walk in the hills together).

★ Follip and Fullop only eat crisps, chips, sweets and cakes. These are foods high in fat, salt and sugar. It is not healthy to only eat these foods.

★ Follip and Fullip need to vary their diet more and include some fruit and vegetables.

Extension activities
★ Pupils could imagine if Follip decided to have a healthier lifestyle but Fullip was stubborn and wanted to continue living an unhealthy lifestyle. How might this affect their friendship and make it harder for Follip to keep his healthy lifestyle?

★ Pupils could use Follip and Fullop as characters in a campaign to try and encourage people to live healthier lifestyles. They could draw persuasive posters that promoted eating fruit and vegetables and exercising.

FOOD WONDERFUL FOOD (PAGE 50)

Purpose of activity: To celebrate the variety of foods.

Key discussion points

★ One of the wonderful things about food is that there is such variety in tastes, textures, the ways it is prepared and cooked and the different combinations that we eat.

★ Learning to enjoy a variety of food tastes can mean people are more likely to have a balanced diet.

★ A balanced diet is not about denying yourself certain foods altogether, it is about eating a mix of food that means you get a variety of nutrients.

★ Too many fatty, salty and sugary foods in the diet would be unhealthy.

Extension activities

★ Pupils can set themselves food challenges e.g. try a new food, eat five fruit and vegetables a day, learn to cook something, replace a salty or sugary snack with an apple, eat all their dinner, drink more water, only eat sweets or crisps once a week ..etc

★ Pupils can list their top three: fruits, vegetables, ice cream flavours, dinners, drinks, ways of eating potato (mashed, chipped, crisps, sauted, roasted, baked, boiled, waffled), foods that come in a tin, sauces, meats, pasta shapes…etc

DIRTY DOFFY (PAGE 51)

Purpose of activity: To consider poor and good personal hygiene.

Key discussion points

★ If a person has poor personal hygiene, it can sometimes be embarrassing to tell them.

★ Poor personal hygiene can have an impact on a person's health – for example not washing hands before eating can spread harmful bacteria or not cleaning teeth can lead to cavities and/or gum disease.

Extension activities

★ Pupils could consider why it is so hard to tell a person that they smell.

★ Pupils could write down the advice Doffy needs to hear as a set of instructions.

★ Pupils could consider the 'tools' needed for

personal hygiene and any advice that could be given about their use. E.g. bath, sink, shower, soap, shampoo, combs and hairbrushes, laundry, handkerchief, toothbrushes e.g. change them about once every 3 months and don't use other people's.

HOW DOES IT MAKE YOU FEEL? (PAGE 52)

Purpose of activity: To develop emotional literacy and consider positive responses to someone being upset.

Activity notes

This activity is best done with pairs of pupils discussing each scenario and agreeing on a 'grading'.

Key discussion points

★ Feelings are feelings and cannot be helped. What we can do, however, is choose how we behave in response to different feelings. Some behaviours (in response to emotions) are more beneficial than others. e.g. when we are angry we might choose to hit someone or we might choose to do something that helps us to calm down.

★ The words positive and negative are used instead of 'good' and 'bad' because it is never a good idea to deny feelings – as the word 'bad' might lead you to believe.

★ Positive feelings can have a positive impact on our behaviour and how we interact with other people.

★ Sometimes, when a person feels a negative emotion, s/he might need to explain assertively how s/he feels and what made him/her feel that way. Sometimes this alone can help people feel better.

★ If a person is upset, it is best to try and be supportive. Sometimes this might mean leaving them alone to cool down and sometimes it might mean being someone who listens.

★ Examples of bad responses to a person being upset are; laughing, teasing them or not taking their upset seriously

Extension activities

★ Pupils could role-play experiencing different negative emotions (they could make up a reason why they feel that way) and consider what would best help them to feel better: e.g. worried, hurt, lonely, miserable, jealous, bored, uncomfortable, embarrassed, scared, rejected, shocked, frustrated, angry…etc it might well be different help for different feelings.

★ Pupils could make posters on the theme of 'things that make me feel great!'

Read about these two very different people and then answer the questions below

RISKY RITA

Rita bounced out of bed and bounded down the stairs. Her dad asked her if she'd like to try the new breakfast cereal. Rita said she would love to.

Rita decided to try taking a slightly different route to school that morning. On the way she saw the new boy, Saif. Rita crossed the road and started to chat to him.

In the playground, Rita's classmates noticed that she was wearing her scruffy old shoes. Rita explained that she'd left her new shoes at home because she'd asked her mum to polish them.

During the register, Rita volunteered to read out the hockey report in assembly, which she later did.

In maths, Rita finished all her work although she wasn't sure if it was all correct. She asked the teacher to mark it for her straight away so she could see if she'd got it right.

At lunchtime Rita ate the olives that her dad had put in her lunch box. She'd never tried olives before. After lunch she joined the korf-ball club, despite the fact that she wasn't sure exactly what it was!

After school, Rita had a go on her friend's scooter because she wanted to know what it was like. Before going to bed, Rita watched a **TV** programme that she didn't usually watch, while one of her favourite programmes was on the other channel.

NO-RISK RICK

Rick went downstairs and asked his mum for his breakfast. He always had cornflakes.

On his way to school that morning, Rick saw the new boy, Saif, but decided not to go and talk to him.

In the playground, he sat on the bench, just like he did every morning.

During the register, Rick read his book. The teacher was asking people if they would help with various jobs but Rick didn't volunteer to do any of them.

At lunchtime Rick had a carrot, a cheese sandwich and a biscuit. This is all he would ever have for his packed lunch. After lunch, he sat on the bench under the oak tree, just like he always did.

During maths, Rick didn't know what to do so he sat quietly in the corner and hoped nobody would notice that he wasn't doing anything. When his friend offered him some help, he shook his head and said he didn't want help.

After school on his way home, Rick's friend asked if he wanted to play round his house next Thursday. Rick said that he did not want to because he had not been there before.

Rick watched his favourite **TV** programme and went to bed.

Read about these two very different people and then answer the questions

1. If taking a risk means doing something when we don't know the outcome, what risks did Rita take?

2. Who do you think had a more interesting day?

3. Why do you think it's sometimes a good idea to take risks?

WHEN WOULD IT BE SAFE?

Write the age at which you think a child or young person would be old enough to do each of the following things safely on their own.

ACTION	AGE
Make a cup of tea.	
Cross the road.	
Use scissors.	
Make toast.	
Be in the bath without an adult looking after them.	
Go on a slide in the park.	
Be left at home alone for an hour.	
Drive a car.	
Be in a back garden with an unfenced pond.	
Be able to reach the medicine cupboard.	
Cycle on the road.	
Use a sharp knife to cut vegetables.	
Go to the park on his/her own.	
Play marbles.	
Babysit a young child.	
Light fireworks.	

Discuss your ideas with a partner or friend. Are the ages you put similar?

PSHE AND CITIZENSHIP 7-9 © MOLLY POTTER 2008

DANGER DETECTIVE

Everyone has to take some risks in their life or they would never do anything. However, a bad risk is putting yourself unnecessarily in a situation where you could possibly be in danger of getting hurt. There are ways of doing things that mean we reduce the chance of something dangerous happening.

1. For each of the following situations, can you detect what the dangers are?
2. Think about the things a person can do to reduce the risk of danger.

CROSSING A VERY BUSY ROAD

Possible dangers:

What could we do to be safer?

CLEARING UP SOME BROKEN GLASS

Possible dangers:

What could we do to be safer?

RIDING A BIKE

Possible dangers:

What could we do to be safer?

AN ADULT DRIVING A CAR

Possible dangers:

What could we do to be safer?

TAKING MEDICINE

Possible dangers:

What could we do to be safer?

COOKING

Possible dangers:

What could we do to be safer?

PSHE AND CITIZENSHIP 7-9 © MOLLY POTTER 2008

Young children need to be taught how to be safe when they are near to a road or crossing one. In the past this has been done in lots of different ways.

Design a campaign that will help teach young children about road safety.

WHAT YOU NEED TO DO

1. Make up a cartoon character that is going to do the road safety teaching.

2. Choose one of the following rules for your character to teach:

★ **Running out into the road without looking is always dangerous.**

★ **It's wise to wear bright clothing if you are near a road after dark.**

★ **To cross the road you need to look both ways and listen before you cross.**

★ **There are some places that make crossing more dangerous e.g. where there are lots of parked cars.**

★ **Using a pedestrian crossing, if there is one, is always a sensible thing to do.**

★ **Look for cyclists when you cross the road as they are easy to miss because they are much quieter than cars.**

★ **Crossing the road near a junction is more dangerous than crossing anywhere else.**

3. **Make up a slogan to help get your message across.**

4. **Make a poster that illustrates your message. Remember to include your slogan and character.**

PSHE AND CITIZENSHIP 7-9 © MOLLY POTTER 2008

A MANUAL FOR MY BODY

Imagine your body came with a manual about how to keep it running healthily. Which of the following sentences do you think would be included?

	WHAT NEEDS TO BE IN THE MANUAL	This would be included in the manual. (Please tick.)
EXERCISING THE BODY	The body doesn't need exercise – it's not important.	
	The body needs to be exercised at least once a week for 5 minutes.	
	Sitting very still is very good exercise for the body.	
	The body needs to be exercised for 30 minutes every day.	
	It's best if the body is exercised non-stop.	
	Pulling faces at people is good exercise.	
WHAT THE BODY EATS	It's good if the body has lots of sugar to eat.	
	It's great if the body gets five portions of fruit or vegetables a day.	
	The body needs to eat fat, but too much fat is not good for it.	
	Food is placed into the ear.	
	The body needs something called roughage (which is found in things like brown bread, fruit and cereals) to make sure its digestive system functions.	
	Too much salt is bad for the body.	
SLEEP	If the body is about 8 years old, it will need about 10 hours sleep a night.	
	Sleep is not needed.	
	Sleep helps the body to repair and feel good.	
	Sleep stops the face from yawning all the time.	
A HEALTHY MIND	If the brain part of the body is worried, talking to someone usually helps it to feel better.	
	Friends help to make the body happy.	
	Laughing is very good for the body.	
	Sleep helps the body to stay happy.	
	You can press the nose to make the body happy.	
	Thinking positively helps to keep the body happy.	
DRINKING FLUID	Petrol is put in the mouth of the body.	
	About 6 or 7 glasses of liquid a day is good for the body.	
	Liquid is very important for the body.	
	Liquid is needed so that the body can squirt enemies.	

FOLLIP AND FULLOP

Here is a picture of Follip and Fullop doing what they like best – watching **TV** in one of their houses while eating a big bowl of chips! They are very good friends.

FOLLIP   **FULLOP**

Fullop and Follip live on the island of Lazil. They both have a car and drive absolutely everywhere, even the **200** metres to each other's houses.

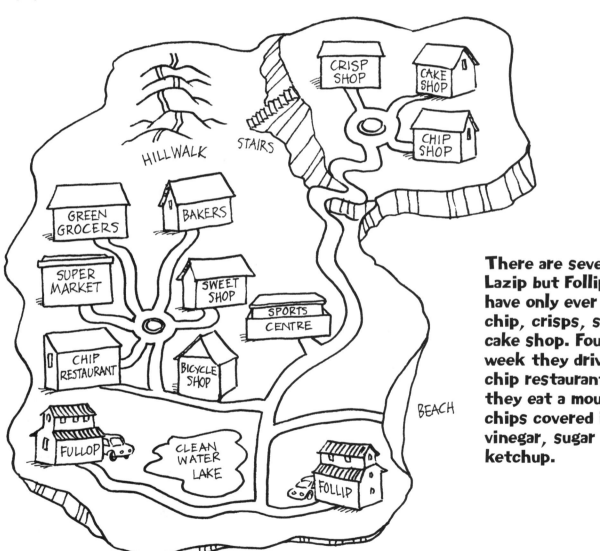

There are several shops on Lazip but Follip and Fullip have only ever been to the chip, crisps, sweet and cake shop. Four times a week they drive to the chip restaurant where they eat a mountain of chips covered in salt, vinegar, sugar and ketchup.

1. What reasons do you think Follip and Fullop would give for having such an unhealthy lifestyle?

2. If you were to meet Follip and Fullop, what would you say to them to try and persuade them to make their lives healthier?

3) Describe how Follip and Fullop might spend their day on Lazil after they have been persuaded to live a healthier lifestyle.

PSHE AND CITIZENSHIP 7-9 © MOLLY POTTER 2008

FOOD, WONDERFUL FOOD

I. If for some reason you were only allowed to eat one of the following foods all day long, which would you choose?

APPLES, CHIPS, CARROTS, BAKED BEANS, READY-SALTED CRISPS, BANANAS, MASHED POTATO

2. What do you think it would be like to eat this food all day long?

3. In this table tick the foods you like.

chips		banana		rice	
raw carrot		pear		fish fingers	
fried egg		baked beans		sausage	
brussel sprouts		apple		pasta	
corn flakes		ham		chocolate	
strawberry jam		yoghurt		beetroot	
marshmallows		cauliflower		toffee	
bread		peas		scrambled egg	
jelly		butter		bacon	
sweetcorn		cheese		marzipan	
oranges		gravy		lettuce	

4. There are loads of different foods and lots of different ways in which they can be cooked. Which of the following would describe what you do when it comes to trying a new food?

VERY DARING
I'll try anything.

DARING
I'll try most things.

QUITE DARING
There are some foods I might not try because I don't like how they look or feel.

NOT VERY DARING
I tend to stick to the foods I know I like.

NOT DARING AT ALL
I never try new foods.

5. Can you think of the last new food you tried and whether you liked it or not?

6. On a separate piece of paper design your perfect dinner menu. Include a main course, a pudding and a drink. Your meal doesn't have to be ordinary. You could mix up lots of food that you like, even if people don't usually have them together.

This is Doffy. Doffy is not very good at personal hygiene. You are going to tell her what she needs to do to clean up her act!

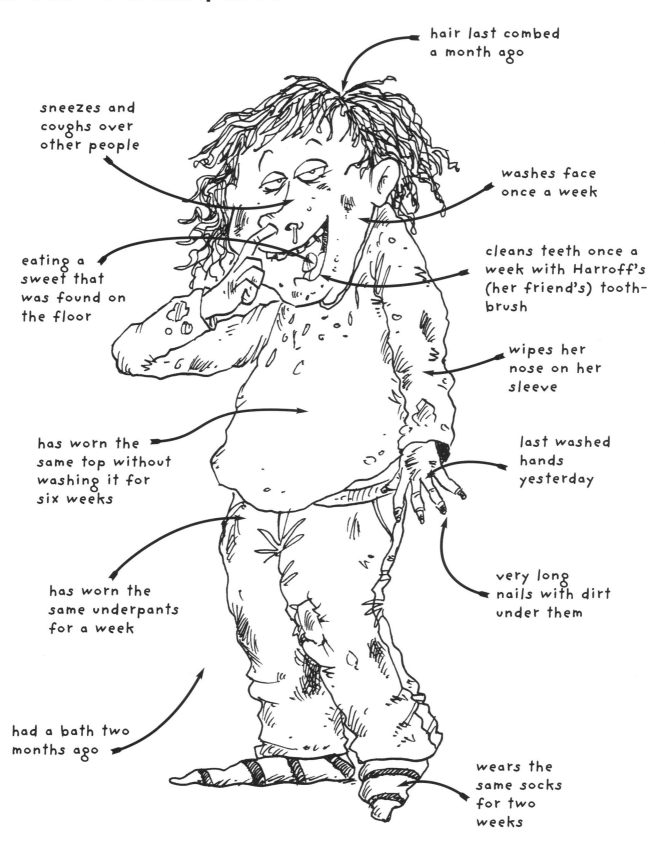

hair last combed a month ago

sneezes and coughs over other people

washes face once a week

eating a sweet that was found on the floor

cleans teeth once a week with Harroff's (her friend's) tooth-brush

wipes her nose on her sleeve

has worn the same top without washing it for six weeks

last washed hands yesterday

has worn the same underpants for a week

very long nails with dirt under them

had a bath two months ago

wears the same socks for two weeks

on the back of this sheet draw a Dirt-free Doffy with better personal hygiene and label what has changed.

PSHE AND CITIZENSHIP 7-9 © MOLLY POTTER 2008

HOW DOES IT MAKE YOU FEEL?

Consider how the following scenarios would make you feel if they happened at school. Label each thing using the key below:

VN	N	O	P	VP
Very negative	**Negative**	**Neither positive nor negative**	**Positive**	**Very positive**

Being hungry or thirsty	Something happening to you that is unfair
A friend not listening to you	Someone asking you what you think about something
Someone smiling at you	Being shown something that makes you laugh
Having too many things to do	Being told why you are a good friend
Finding work too difficult	Not getting a turn on something
Getting praise for something you've done	Being told off for something you didn't do
Doing a piece of work you are proud of	Being persuaded to do something you don't want to do
Losing something	Someone asking you to play with them
Being teased	Someone laughing at you when you are hurt or upset
Being unable to concentrate	Getting good at something you once couldn't do
Being too hot or too cold	Someone hitting you

1. When you are feeling positive, how are you likely to behave?

2. When you are feeling negative, how are you likely to behave?

3. If someone is upset, what do you think would be...

    ★ the best thing to do?
    ★ the worst thing to do?

PSHE AND CITIZENSHIP 7-9 © MOLLY POTTER 2008

THE WORLD AROUND US

RULES TO HELP POOR MELVIN! (PAGE 56)

Purpose of the activity: To develop 'ground rules' for a class so that everyone feels included, safe to participate and able to learn.

Key discussion points

★ Ground rules aim to make everyone feel safe and secure in a learning setting. If people don't feel secure, they are much less likely to learn.

★ Pupils will come up with a variety of rules such as:
1. If someone asks for feedback – if you think it could be improved – make suggestions, do not just criticise.
2. Try to make sure everyone feels included.
3. You can always ask questions – even if you think you should know the answer.
4. Only one person should speak at a time.
5. No put downs.
6. If you upset someone, make sure you apologise and take their upset seriously.
7. Aim to make sure everyone gets a go at talking.
8. Listen well to each other.
9. Encourage each other.
10. If someone is struggling, help them.
11. Have fun – without ruining other people' concentration – it's good for learning.
12. Make sure people can concentrate if they need to. Respect everyone's right to learn.

Extension activities

★ Pupils could describe how they would have felt at each significant point in the story if they had been Melvin.

★ Pupils could draw two contrasting cartoon pictures – one illustrating all the ground rules being followed by a class and another where they are not followed. They could discuss why one is so much better than the other.

★ Pupils could order the ground rules from the rule they consider to be most important to the least.

★ Pupils could discuss a way of monitoring how well the ground rules are followed.

A WELCOME POLICY (PAGE 57)

Purpose of activity: To empathise with new pupils and visitors and consider how to make them welcome in school.

Key discussion points

★ Pupils could work in groups to consider and develop a variety of actions and ideas that would make a person feel welcome: e.g. smiles, good manners, chatting to the person, making sure they know where things like the toilets are, offering a drink, explaining things, checking to see if they need anything and that they are OK.

★ It is a good idea to include practical notions in a policy which everyone could realistically stick to.

Extension activities

★ Pupils could design a welcome mat or welcome poster for the school.

★ Pupils could make a welcome pack for new pupils.

A HAPPY OR MISERABLE SCHOOL (PAGE 58)

Purpose of activity: To consider the factors that contribute towards a school's wellbeing.

Key discussion points

★ A positive environment is made with a combination of components: the physical surroundings, how positive interactions are between the people; fairness, the relationships that form between people and structures that make people feel safe and know what to expect.

★ A simple way of thinking about this issue is to ask pupils what a happy school looks, feels and sounds like.

Extension activities
★ Pupils could write a Happy School Policy.

★ Pupils could write as many sentence ends as they can think of for the start, 'A happy school....'

★ Pupils could develop a happiness questionnaire that explores how people feel at different times in the school day.

★ Pupils could draw a happiness map indicating the parts of the school in which they feel most happy.

★ Pupils could focus in further on an unhappy and happy classroom, lesson or break time - and write the ingredients for a happy classroom etc.

★ Pupils could write six statements about what they think would make their school an even happier place.

THE SCHOOL LIBRARY (PAGE 59)
Purpose of activity: To consider how to fairly decide to allocate money for resources and to develop ideas for how the library could be improved.

Key discussion points
★ Pupils might decide to have a competition to develop ideas for how to improve the library then ask the whole school to vote on which improvements they would prefer.

★ Improvements might include: comfortable seating, a table, paint the wall, a mural, a carpet, a rug, duplicated versions of very popular books, a 'recommendations' shelf, more lighting, posters for the wall, get rid of the old books that no one reads to make more space for seating, a plan to show where you find different types of book, a new library sign, a quiz that people can find all the answers for in the library, block off one door to make a cosy corner etc.

Extension activities
★ Pupils could design a mural they think would be appropriate for a library.

★ Pupils could draw a plan and a photograph of a super library.

★ Pupils could make posters that encourage people to use the new improved library.

FUNDRAISING (PAGE 60)
Purpose of activity: To consider different ways to raise money and how easy or difficult they would be to carry out.

Key discussion points
★ Most people are usually prepared to give money to a cause if they think it is a good one. People usually like to see that an effort has been made to coax the money out of them! The more interesting the event, the more likely it is to make money.

★ If pupils aim their fundraising event at adults, they are likely to make more money.

★ Some examples of events are: a competition with a prize - that costs to enter (e.g. a decorate your friend, guess the name of the teddy, design a lesson competition, a treasure hunt , make a vegetable pet, guess who the baby is, design a playground game, an observation quiz) a raffle with prizes that have been donated by local businesses, a quiz night for parents/carers, a selection of bring and buy stalls, a soak the teacher stall, a non-uniform day, a dress as your teacher day, a come to school with your child day etc.

Extension activities
★ Pupils could imagine having £200 to spend on their playground. They could discuss how the money could be spent (paint for a mural, playground equipment, benches, shelter, garden, patterns painted onto the ground etc)

★ Pupils could make posters to advertise their made up event. With this poster, they could consider how they could make people care about their cause.

YOUR JOURNEY TO SCHOOL – SCAVENGER HUNT (PAGE 61)
Purpose of activity: To increase awareness of the local community.

Key discussion points
★ Pupils could be set this for homework.

★ The most likely laws pupils will be aware of are traffic laws.

★ A sign that someone has not been responsible could be something as simple as litter.

Extension activities
★ Pupils could draw a map of their route to school and label the positions where they spotted each thing. They could also add further examples of each thing as they see more.

★ Pupils could make up their own scavenger hunt with a theme: e.g. safety, responsibilities, rules, emotions, learning etc

LITTER IN HILLTOP PARK (PAGE 62)

Purpose of the activity: To consider how to persuade people to change their habits and care about Hilltop Park.

Key discussion points

★ For people to change their habits, they need to be made to think about what they are doing.

★ If people consider what the park could be like, they might start to take pride in it.

★ Features of the park could be used to be persuasive e.g. pictures of children playing happily in a litter-free park or families having a picnic in the picnic area.

Extension activities

★ Pupils could draw a before and after photograph of an area of the park.

★ Pupils could consider other things they could do to prevent litter. For example, hold a 'celebration of the park' fair, hold meetings in the park to discuss the problem, make leaflets persuading people to take pride in the park, involve local school children in litter patrols.

ALL PACKAGED UP (PAGE 63)

Purpose of activity: To consider the over-use of packaging and how to persuade people it's not necessary.

Key discussion points

★ A lot of packaging is used to make a product look really appealing to increase the likelihood of someone deciding to buy it. A lot of this packaging is not actually necessary for protecting or containing the product.

★ In the western world a lot of packaging ends up in landfill sites. These sites are filling up.

★ Packaging can often be recycled but this is not as good as not using it in the first place.

★ Any advertising to promote a toy with less packaging could focus on:

    a) no need to battle with the packaging to get it out and

    b) less waste produced.

Extension activities

★ Pupils could look how a variety of products are packaged and consider which elements are practical and which are cosmetic.

★ Pupils could write a letter trying to persuade a company to use less packaging on their products.

★ Pupils could design a food shop that aims to keep its packaging to a minimum and consider how the shop would do this.

WOULD YOU BELIEVE IT? (PAGE 64)

Purpose of activity: To consider how adverts exaggerate and to develop a discerning eye for the media.

Key discussion points

★ The odd advert out is for toothpaste because it just states what the toothpaste does without even attempting to make it sound fantastic.

★ Any advert's sole purpose is to try and get people to buy the product.

★ These example adverts use slogans and exaggerate by using describing words and making slightly unrealistic claims – such as 'you'll never want to use another tea bag again.'

Extension activities

★ Pupils could look at more examples of adverts and consider what each advert is doing to try and persuade you to buy the product. (e.g. using eye-catching pictures, grabbing your attention with a question, making you seem stylish if you buy the product, making you feel guilty if you don't. etc)

★ Pupils could re-write the three realistic adverts on the sheet to make the product sound ordinary.

Read the passage, 'I didn't have a good day' and underline all the parts where Melvin was made to feel bad or uncomfortable. Write down some rules that would prevent Melvin from feeling the way he did if everyone decided to follow them.

HERE'S A RULE TO START YOU OFF:
★ If someone asks for feedback, make sure it's positive. If you think there's room for improvement make suggestions, don't just criticise.

I DIDN'T HAVE A GOOD DAY

Melvin entered the classroom. Everyone stared at him. Poppy and Brian whispered something to each other.

Melvin sat down at his desk. Jane sat next to him but she had her back turned to him. When Jane turned round, she made a joke about how messy his hair was. When Melvin said, 'that doesn't make me feel very good,' Jane just laughed at him.

During break time, Melvin couldn't find anyone to talk to at first. Eventually Jordan came over to talk to him but Jordan just went on and on about the football team and Melvin felt he couldn't really get a word in.

During maths, Melvin got in a muddle and when he asked his friend Larry a question, Larry laughed at him for not knowing the answer. Melvin then tried asking the teacher, Mr Phelps, but he was dismissive and appeared not to understand what it was Melvin was finding difficult. Mr Phelps also talked over Melvin as he asked the question. Melvin decided to just sit there and do nothing until the end of the lesson. He felt he couldn't concentrate anyway as Patricia and Nathan were messing around so loudly on the next table.

Things started looking up in history as Melvin drew a storyboard of the Battle of Hastings but then Mr Phelps told him that he was having too much fun and he needed to finish it more quickly and get on with the writing. He asked Mr Phelps if he liked the drawing but he said he thought it was just messy.

PSHE AND CITIZENSHIP 7-9 © MOLLY POTTER 2008

WHAT IS A POLICY?

A policy is a piece of paper that lists what everyone has agreed to do about something. Schools have lots of policies e.g. a school will have an anti-bullying policy which tells everyone what the school will do about bullying if it happens.

Imagine a new pupil was starting at your school or an adult was visiting the school to come and talk in an assembly. How might these people feel? What could everyone in school do to make sure that both people were made to feel welcome?

You are going to write a welcome policy. This policy will explain all the things that will happen in your school to make visitors or new pupils feel very welcome.

HERE ARE SOME HEADING IDEAS THAT YOU COULD USE IN YOUR POLICY:

MAKING A VISITOR FEEL WELCOME
- ★ When a visitor first arrives – where do they go?
- ★ How is the visitor greeted?
- ★ Finding out what a visitor needs
- ★ Refreshments
- ★ Showing the visitor around
- ★ Manners
- ★ Smiling

MAKING A NEW PUPIL FEEL WELCOME
- ★ What needs to happen to make the new pupil feel welcome?
- ★ Being introduced to the class
- ★ Showing the pupil around the school
- ★ Answering the pupil's questions
- ★ Helping the pupil to make friends
- ★ Checking how the pupil feels
- ★ Making sure the pupil has the information s/he needs

PSHE AND CITIZENSHIP 7-9 © MOLLY POTTER 2008

A HAPPY OR SAD SCHOOL

In the town of **Mixton** there are two primary schools: Joy Valley Primary School where the pupils are always happy and Sad Valley Primary School where the pupils are always miserable. Complete the following table with likely reasons why the pupils in each school feel the way they do. Use the titles in the table to help you think about this.

	JOY VALLEY PRIMARY SCHOOL	SAD VALLEY PRIMARY SCHOOL
How the pupils treat each other		
Classrooms		
Teachers		
Lessons		
Playtimes		
Lunch		
Other reasons		

Discuss with a partner what you think makes a happy school.

£500 has been given to Gretton Primary School library and the school council has been asked to decide how it will be spent.

At the moment, the library is very well stocked with new books. It also has a large number of old and rather tatty books. It's not a particularly pleasant place to be because of the lack of seating. The walls are painted grey. In one corner, there is a tatty poster showing the colour coding of the Dewey system.

This is a plan of the library.

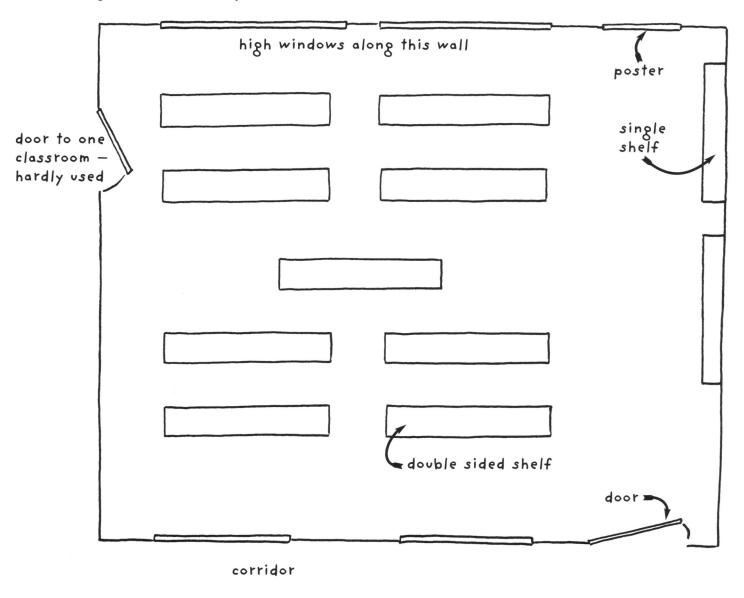

high windows along this wall

poster

single shelf

door to one classroom — hardly used

double sided shelf

door

corridor

PSHE AND CITIZENSHIP 7-9 © MOLLY POTTER 2008

YOUR TASK

1. How do you think the school council should decide what to do with the money?
2. If you were deciding what to spend the money on, what would you choose?
3. What else could you do that doesn't cost any, or hardly any, money to improve the library?

FUNDRAISING

Joan is the chairperson of the school council.

If Joan raises £100, her headteacher will give her another £100 towards making the playground a better place.

What could Joan do to raise £100?

One example has been completed for you. Can you complete the table with more ideas?

IDEAS	PROS	CONS	EASINESS mark out of ten (0 easy, 10 difficult)
Persuade pupils to bring in their old toys and set up a stall to sell them at break time	It won't cost much to set up.	It might be hard to make the full amount of money.	2
Organise a sponsored walk			

Which idea do you think is best and why?

PSHE AND CITIZENSHIP 7-9 © MOLLY POTTER 2008

YOUR JOURNEY TO SCHOOL

On your journey to or from school, look out for the following things. It might take more than one journey to see them all. If your journey is very short, you might have to think of another route near to your home that you take. Draw or describe each thing as you find them.

Something that happens because it is law e.g. cars drive on the left side of the road.	**A person being responsible for or about something or someone.**
Something that shows someone has not been responsible.	**Something a person did to keep themselves or other people safe.**
Something that shows a person is looking after their house.	**A place that lots of different people go to.**
A sign that gives people information.	**Something that looks like it needs repairing or a coat of paint.**

PSHE AND CITIZENSHIP 7-9 © MOLLY POTTER 2008

Hilltop Park could be lovely but it isn't! The reason for this is litter. For some reason people have just got used to throwing their litter on the ground even though there are plenty of litter bins. The local council is not happy about the amount of time and money they have to spend clearing up the litter and have decided to do something about it. They have asked you to help put a stop to the litter problem in Hilltop Park by designing an eye-catching poster.

Here is a map of the park

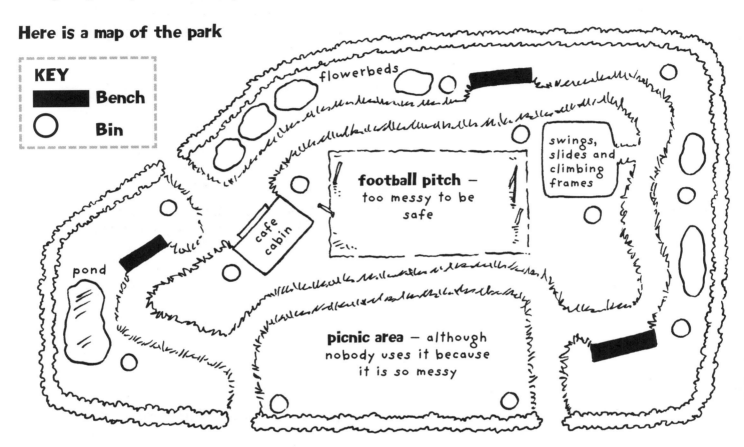

MORE INFORMATION

★ Very few children play games in the park because it's not a nice place to be.

★ No one sits on the benches because the view is so awful.

★ Nobody has ever had a picnic in the park. There are several picnic benches in the picnic area but the whole area is a mess.

★ People do use the park for walking their dogs but they don't bother tidying up any mess the dog makes.

★ The Cabin Café only sells tea to dog walkers.

★ The pond is full of litter even though it has a few goldfish in it.

★ Before the posters go up, the park will be thoroughly cleaned and given a bit of a makeover.

WHAT YOU NEED TO DO

Make a poster that will be put up in and around the park. The poster needs to make people want to keep Hilltop Park litter free. You need to consider what would really make people change their habits and start using the bins. It won't be enough just to say – use the bins!

A toy company has decided to use less packaging with its toys so that they are more 'green'.

This is what a typical toy looks like when it is packaged up.

This is what the same toy will look like with the new 'green' policy in place.

Here are some comments people have made about packaging for toys:

"I know that when my son is in a toy shop he's more likely to grab a toy if it looks good and he can see clearly what it is."

"When my children open their birthday presents, they're always disappointed with how long it takes to actually get to the toy because of all the packaging."

"When you remove all the packaging, the toy looks so much smaller and then you have to get rid of so much rubbish — it fills up our recycling bin."

The company is worried that the new packaging will make the toy so much less interesting to look at and therefore people won't buy it. What do you think they can do to make sure people still buy their toys?

They have asked you to make an advert that will persuade people to buy their toys **BECAUSE** they use so much less packaging. How will you persuade people to do this?

PSHE AND CITIZENSHIP 7-9 © MOLLY POTTER 2008

Look at these adverts.

SUDSY SOAP
Soap that washes like magic.

Sudsy soap will clean your children like no other soap.
Children love it - they will beg to be bathed!

BRIGHT'S
TOOTHPASTE

Toothpaste for cleaning your teeth with a brush.
Mint flavoured – much like all other toothpastes.

FABOOS
Make life sweeter!

The most amazing sweets you are ever likely to taste. Save the time you usually spend choosing sweets – try these once and you'll never choose another sweet!
FABOOS come in delicious chocolate, scrumptious strawberries and cream, and yummy banana flavours.

TIP TOP TEA BAGS
YOU'LL NEVER WANT TO USE ANOTHER TEABAG.

Tip Top Tea Bags' special lining ensures the full flavour of our tea is delivered to your cup every time.

TALK ABOUT
★ Which advert is the odd one out?
★ What do adverts try to get you to do?
★ How do adverts try to persuade you to buy what they are advertising?

Adverts are not allowed to lie but they can exaggerate. Is there anything in these adverts that you wouldn't believe?

PSHE AND CITIZENSHIP 7-9 © MOLLY POTTER 2008